SOURCE OF ALL EVIL
AFRICAN PROVERBS AND SAYINGS ON WOMEN

Also by Mineke Schipper:

Beyond the Boundaries: African Literature and Literary Theory (1989)

SOURCE
OF ALL EVIL

AFRICAN PROVERBS
AND SAYINGS ON WOMEN

MINEKE SCHIPPER

Ivan R. Dee
Chicago

To Ama Ata Aidoo, Micere Githae Mugo and Miriam Tlali,
Daughters, Mothers, Writers.

SOURCE OF ALL EVIL. Copyright © 1991 by Mineke Schipper.
All rights reserved, including the right to reproduce this book or
portions thereof in any form. For information, address: Ivan R. Dee,
Inc., 1332 North Halsted Street, Chicago 60622. First American edition.

Library of Congress Cataloguing-in-Publication Data:
Schipper, Mineke.
   Source of all evil : African proverbs and sayings on women /
Mineke Schipper.
      p.   cm.
   Includes bibliographical references and index.
   ISBN 0–929587–73–1
   1. Proverbs, African.   2. Women–Quotations, maxims, etc.
I. Title
PN6519.A6S28   1991
398.9′096–dc20   91–14605

Printed in Great Britain

Woman is the source of all evil;
only our soul saves us from the
harm she does.

(*Fon, Benin*)

CONTENTS

Contents

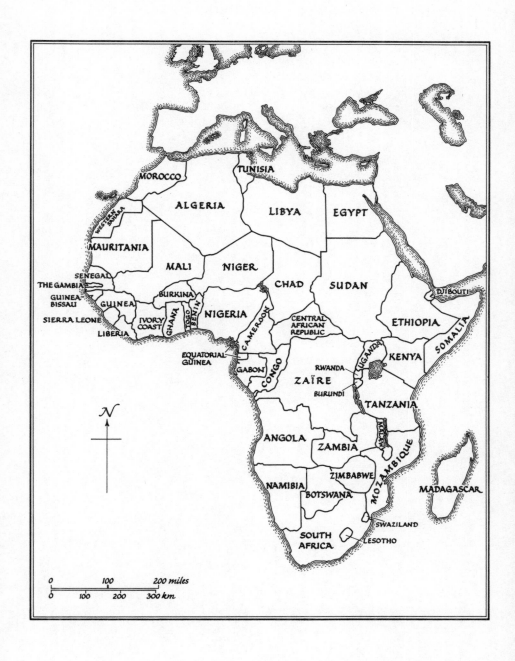

INTRODUCTION

PROVERBS AND WOMEN

"One who applies proverbs gets what s/he
wants."
(*Shona, Zimbabwe*)

Although no satisfactory all-embracing definition exists, proverbs
are recognized as such by users and listeners, when quoted in a
specific context. One might describe them as short pithy sayings,
ingeniously embodying an admitted truth or common belief. Defi-
nitions generally emphasize three characteristics of the proverb:
(1) its concise fixed artistic form; (2) its evaluative and conservative
function in society; (3) its authoritive validity.

Proverbs on Proverbs

The motto to this introduction is a proverb on proverbs. There are
many of them, underlining the fact that proverbs are powerful and
therefore to be taken seriously. They can be found in very different
places: "A hundred proverbs – a hundred truths" (Spain); "An old
proverb will never break" (Russia); "All proverbs walk upon stilts"
(Sweden); "A proverb is the ornament of speech" (Iran, Meier-
Pfaller, 1980: 14f). And: "Proverbs are the cream of language"
(Afar); "A speech without proverb is food without salt" (Amharic,
Ethiopia); "Proverbs are the horses of speech" (Yoruba, Nigeria).
This last proverb means that if communication gets lost, proverbs
are used to retrieve it. Readers in the West perhaps believe that
proverbs are no longer alive in their society, but the *Penguin Dictionary*

1

of Proverbs (1986: 197) reminds of their lasting impact: "Though the proverb is abandoned, it is not falsified."

Let us now look at the way proverbs affect oral communication.

Proverbs as Quotes

Whether they come from the Koran, the Bible, political leaders, popes, patriarchs, philosophers, poets, or traditional wisdom, proverbs and sayings are quotes used to give credence to the speaker. Their sources are considered experts. In an oral culture, the experts are – mainly or exclusively – chiefs, elders and ancestors, as specialists on tradition and as its representatives or symbols.

A proverb acquires its concrete meaning only when it is used: "In the absence of the situation there is no proverb"(Brookman-Amissah, 1971/72: 264). New shades of meaning may develop in new situations. For instance, a poor man who complains about his misery might quote the following saying: "Whether the widow has her period or not does not make any difference" (Baule, Ivory Coast). In his society, it means, literally, that a widow has no right to have sexual intercourse, and neither does a woman who has her period. In this man's particular situation, it means that whether it is a festive day or an ordinary day makes no difference to the poor, since their situation is always the same. The example makes clear that an originally simple straightforward saying with a literal meaning may become metaphorical and thus applicable to other situations. Sometimes it is used in both ways by the same community.

For our purpose, sayings literally referring to women as well as metaphorical ones have been collected, since the two categories tell us about women in the society concerned. Proverbs benefit people who know how to make good use of them. The Czech scholar Jan Mukarovsky wrote an essay on the proverb in context. He coined the term "quoting behaviour". Quotations are used "to indicate something that the speaker for whatever reason does not wish to say out directly" (Mukarovsky, 1971: 299). Joyce Penfield published a study on quoting behaviour, particularly with respect to proverbs, among the Igbo of Nigeria. She applied and elaborated upon Mukarovsky's observations, and recommended further research on possible cross-cultural universal properties of quoting behaviour (Penfield, 1983: 4). It would certainly be interesting to see the results of more comparitive research on the manipulatory effect of proverbs with respect to gender relations in various societies.

Introduction

In any oral communication situation, a *speaker* addresses a *message* to one or more *listeners* in a particlar *context*. This also holds for the quoted proverb: it allows the *speaker* to broach sensitive matters in an abstract and indirect manner, "desubjectivized" in Mukarovsky's words. As a matter of fact, indirectness is a highly esteemed quality in many oral societies. Thus, the speaker is not held personally responsible for his/her statement. It can serve to protect someone using proverbs as criticism or mockery or insults.

The use of proverbs gives the speaker prestige. In oral cultures, people are impressed by those who have many proverbs at their disposal and know how to use them at the right moment. The audience's moral acceptance of the proverbs strengthens the speaker's message: the proverb is associated with the authority of wisdom. Referring to the wisdom's unquestioned validity, the speaker deserves respect and authority himself. Communicating with quotes is an art and a source of prestige for people who know how to display their ability and maturity in the use of proverbs. The man who exhibits his wisdom confirms traditional values and the existing power relations. Thus, he "gets what he wants".

The effect of the literary device of "singularization" or of "de-automatization" (Sklovski, 1966: 84) is to highlight the proverb's *message* through devices such as rhythm, rhyme, assonance, alliteration, parallelism, metaphor, inversion, contrast and so forth. Each use of a well-known proverb in a new speech situation makes it attract renewed attention.

The user of proverbs appeals to the *listeners'* norms and values, traditionally shared by the cultural *context*, the community they belong to: "Both collective acceptance and traditionality are the consequences of socialization of certain forms of expression which originally must have been individual. Collective acceptance here, however, as opposed to traditionality which is passive, seems to be an active factor: something that has achieved social acceptance is not only generally used but also generally accepted as correct." (Mukarovsky, 1971: 295)

Proverbs on Women: A Global Phenomenon

As part of a people's cultural heritage, proverbs are embedded in the context in which they function. By their very nature, they confirm societal norms and values. Anthropologists rightly state that studying peoples' proverbs means getting to know them better. Of course, one has to be careful not to jump too easily to conclusions about *the* image of women in society. First of all, it is indispensable to take into account

3

that readers are not necessarily insiders, which should at least inspire in us a good dose of modesty. Secondly, proverbs are not isolated sayings: they function in a complex social and cultural context. Still, proverbs of most cultures have certain things in common, for instance that their impact is oral rather than written.

As for the content, in spite of different cultural and geographical origins, a number of similar traits are attributed to women in proverbs. I first realized this when working on *Unheard Words: Women and Literature in Africa, the Arab World, Asia, the Caribbean and Latin America* (1985). Each section in that book was prefaced by a small selection of proverbs from the area. It struck me that the only category of women favourably portrayed in these proverbs was the mother – unique, loving, reliable, hard-working, and therefore: "A wife should be like one's mother" (Swahili, **I**. V, 2). None the less, the mother often seems to prefer sons to daughters: "No matter how beautiful and talented a girl is, a boy – even deformed – is always more valuable" (China, in: Schipper, 1985: 123). As far as other women are concerned, they are more unfaithful than virtuous, and men are warned again and again not to fall for their charms and evil intentions: "Like the scorpion, woman is a relative of the devil: when she sees a poor wretch, she wiggles her behind and moves away" (Uruguay, *ibid.*: 212). "A good wife, an injured leg and a pair of torn trousers stay at home" (Netherlands/Spain). The silent submissive type is highly recommended: "Virtuous is the girl who suffers and dies without a sound" (India, *ibid.*: 122). Another point often stressed is that women ought to be less clever and in fact should be (kept) inferior to men in general and to their husbands in particular: "A woman who knows Latin will neither find a husband nor come to a good end" (Argentina) or: "Never marry a woman with bigger feet than your own" (Sena, Malawi/Mozambique, *ibid.*: 212, 21).

These examples give a first impression of proverbs on women from different countries. In the introduction to the *Penguin Dictionary of Proverbs* (1986: vi), it is said that proverbs "do not have to be true", since they sometimes contradict each other. In proverbs on women this is sometimes the case; for example, the issue of monogamy can be looked at differently. However, it seems to me that the issue of the perspective they represent is much more important, although hardly studied. With regard to gender in proverbs (but in fact with regard to all kinds of texts), the following questions are relevant: Who is quoting? Whose views are presented? Who is subject and who is object? Who profits from the impact such quotations have? Whose is the general consensus referred to? Whose power is perpetuated, at the expense of whom? With the quote, the speaker gives a value judgement. The proverb's authority and its evaluative nature exhort the listener to agree. Although there are cases where the authoritative aspect of the proverb is not so much stressed, in many proverbs on women it apparently plays a role.

The question of what anthropology has to say about women has been asked for about two decades. It has indeed meant a new perspective on many issues in the field and new insights into the (power) relations of men and women. As Rosaldo and Lamphere put it in their study on *Women, Culture and Society* (1985: 3):

> The current anthropological view draws on the observation that most and probably all contemporary societies, whatever their kinship organization or mode of subsistence, are characterized by some degree of male dominance . . . none has observed a society in which women have publicly recognized power and authority surpassing that of men. Everywhere we find that women are excluded from certain crucial economic or political activites, that their roles as wives and mothers are associated with fewer powers and prerogatives than are the roles of men. It seems fair to say, then, that all contemporary societies are to some extent male-dominated, and although the degree and expression of female subordination vary greatly, sexual asymmetry is presently a universal fact of human social life.

Indeed, the majority of proverbs seem to underline the authority of the quotes and implicitly of their users, whose perspective can sometimes be identified as male. To give an example, women cannot logically quote the following proverb: "Woman is the source of all evil; only our soul saves us from the harm she does" (Fon, Benin).

When authors talk about the general consensus on proverbs and their objectivity as a source of information, they often idealize, nostalgically and romantically, their eternal truth, indestructible roots and indispensable wisdom, as guards of social harmony and good conduct. For the time being, it seems justified to ask some questions on the speaker's (gender) perspective and interests before taking the general consensus for granted.

Given the changes among women and societies, a number of proverbs no longer reflect certain women's realities today, particularly in the urban areas. Still, many proverbs in many cultures continue to represent deep-rooted ideas on women's roles and (im)possibilities. Where the proverbs are no longer quoted, these ideas do not seem to disappear naturally at the same time. Internalized images, collective memories and traditions are handed down from one generation to the next and are fundamental to the construction of people's everyday realities, where the emphasis on woman's maternal role has led to what Rosaldo (1985: 8) explained as:

> a universal opposition between "domestic" and "public" roles that is necessarily asymmetrical; women, confined to the domestic sphere, do not have access to the sorts of authority, prestige, and cultural value that are the prerogatives of men . . . Given this imbalance, the exercise of power by women is often seen as illegitimate, and the avenues by which women gain prestige and a sense of value are shaped and often limited by their association with the domestic world.

This fascinating book on proverbs will serve as a source of documentation and a stimulus for further research and discussion. The proverbs represent material on the interaction between male and female, personal and collective, identities in different cultures and societies. But, first of all, they constitute fascinating reading for everyone interested in woman's roles – accepted, despised, prescribed, past or present – and in her daily struggle for survival in a materially, socially and culturally still often restrictive world.

WOMEN AND PROVERBS
IN AFRICA

Africa is famous for its proverbs, where countless proverbs are alive and popular, colourful and striking, and those on women pre-eminently so.

Classification

African proverbs can be roughly divided into (a) clear, direct statements, i.e. moral sayings or mottoes, and (b) proverbs in meta-phorical form. Examples are: (a) "Women have no mouth" (Beti, **II**. X, 24); (b) "The hen knows when it is morning, but she looks at the mouth of the cock" (= she waits for the cock to crow; Ashanti, **II**. X, 27). In their application, the direct ones may become metaphorical, as in the above quoted Baule example on the widow. In the terminology of African languages, a real distinction is not always made between the two, as Ruth Finnegan (1970: 390f) observed. For further information on this and many other aspects of African proverbs, I recommend the excellent chapter on the subject in her book *Oral Literature in Africa* (1970).

It is impossible to provide a completely satisfactory classification of proverbs. They always overlap in a number of ways, and this book is no exception. Although Part **I**, *Phases of Life*, contains ten clearly different categories of womankind, a woman can be a wife, a daughter, a mother or a grandmother, or all of them at the same time. It all depends on relations. As one proverb says: "One man's wife is another man's grandmother" (Fula, **I**. IX, 6).

In Part **II**, *Elements of Life*, it is still more complicated: girls, wives, mothers indiscriminately become lovers, workers, quarrellers, poisoners and sisters of the devil. And then, a poisoner can be pregnant or sterile; a lover beautiful and unreliable, a witch quarrelsome and powerful. In other words: quite a few proverbs would certainly fit under several headings. There is no real solution to this problem, except perhaps to include one and the same proverb in different categories, but that would be a drawback for the reader.

In collections of proverbs, women are usually classified under "family" or "human relations", with certain aspects under "miscell-aneous". Examining the classification in other collections, I have found some very curious cases. To give one example, C. E. J. Whitting divided his book *Hausa and Fulani Proverbs* (1935) as follows: (A) Nature; (B) Man; (C) Crafts and Trades; (D) Religion and Conduct. Under (B) Man, we then find "The Family: a. Parents and Children", to end with "b. Others: Wives, Slaves." What does he mean to suggest?

For anyone who would like to order the proverbs by language or country: (if they are known) both are mentioned in brackets after each proverb and in the index. In a few rare cases, it has been impossible to trace the original language and only the country is mentioned. Some languages are spoken on both sides of a frontier, or even in more than one neighbouring country. In spite of this, only one of these countries is mentioned, if it has been explicitly given by the source or informant. Often, however, only the language is mentioned and no country. In these cases, the names of the countries where the language is spoken are indicated. Swahili is an extreme example; it is spoken in various East African countries, from Tanzania, Kenya, Uganda to Zaïre, Rwanda and Burundi. If the exact geographical origin of the Swahili proverb is lacking, East Africa is given as geographical reference. On the other hand, a proverb may exist in more than one language. This is not so surprising, since proverbs travel with their users. On rare occasions, the same proverb is found in different cultures without any demonstrable outside influence or contact.

All in all, this collection contains some six hundred proverbs on women, from all the countries south of the Sahara and more than seventy languages.

"Non-verbal" Proverbs

Proverbs are mainly verbally transmitted, but they have also been expressed through various other media: visually sculpted on wooden boards or pot-lids, engraved in calabashes or woven in cloth, and as symbols in many other art forms. Some peoples in Central Africa use the proverb cord to visualize and teach proverbs to the children.

8

Introduction

This cord is a liane to which all kinds of objects are attached – a chicken leg, herbs, a piece of cloth, and so on. Each object represents a proverb and the cord is used as an educational tool. Another kind of non-verbal transmission of proverbs is musical, by talking drums (Carrington, 1949), horns or trumpets (Nketia, 1979).

A very original case of non-verbal communication of proverbs by women is certainly the Fiote pot-lid message. The Fiote live partly in Cabinda, an Angolan enclave, and partly in Zaïre along the coast. Pot-lids are used by women to indicate truths they would not be permitted to express verbally to their husbands. The lids are round boards with a diameter of about 18 cm. On the top side, images have been sculpted in relief. Each image expresses a proverb or saying. Traditionally, wife and husband do not eat together; the clan's men eat together under the clan penthouse roof. The wives put the food for their husbands in an earthen pot, cover it with a piece of banana leaf and call a child to bring it to the men's place. This is what normally happens. However, if a woman does not agree with her husband's behaviour or if they have a quarrel, she chooses a meaningful proverb pot-lid from her collection or orders an artist to make a new one according to her instructions. As soon as the food with the sculpted cover arrives, the commotion is visible: What, a special pot-lid? Whose is it and what does it mean? The husband has to confess what the problem is and a palaver starts. About his laziness, his impotence, his avarice, the wife's frigidity or her objections to his taking a second wife. If he says he does not understand, the pot-lid is decoded by the specialist and the man is advised by his fellow males. The relief may, for example, show a cooking-pot on three stones. The proverb depicted is: "Three stones support the cooking-pot; three rights a woman has in marriage" (namely clothing, food, sex). The wife's message is that she has complaints about one or more of these marital rights (cf. Vissers, 1982: 21). Sometimes a woman also sends a sculpted message to a woman friend who is angry at her. Thus the woman has a very special means of communication with some unique advantages. For instance, she avoids her husband's initial outburst of rage, since she is not there when her message arrives. He, on the other hand, can moderate his reaction in the presence of other male members of the clan (Vissers, 1982: 13). The pot-lid communication shows that women broach delicate subjects concerning their husbands in a very indirect and subtle way, if at all. Many of the proverbs in this book make it clear that "No woman is called upon to speak" (Rwanda, **II**. X, 25).

Source of all Evil

Proverbial Characteristics

In some proverbs, a truth or moral statement is conveyed with direct *similes*: "Woman is like the earth, everyone sits down on her" (Lingala, **I**. II, 1a). Others display *metaphors*, for example: "A little string binds a big parcel" (Ngbaka, **II**. X, 2a). It applies to a small man marrying a big woman, but also, more generally, confirms that the smallest of the strong is more powerful than the biggest of the weak.

A favourite means of expressive imagination is *personification*. Human qualities are attributed to animals, as in the proverb quoted on the hen and the cock. Objects can reason, think or act: "A mother's back sins when it is seated" (Rundi, **II**. VI, 3). One finds *exaggerations*: "A thousand wives, a thousand palavers" (Ashanti, **I**. IV, 31) and *euphemisms*, e.g. on the risks of multiple female sexual partners: "Not all little seats are good to occupy" (Mandinka, **II**. III, 21a), or to enwrap a negative comment, like the one referring to a sterile woman as "a calabash out of use, its cork being too tight" (Van Roy and Daeleman, 1963: 18), or to a woman's unfaithfulness as "a cluster of palm nuts" (Baule, **II**. VIII, 22).

Many proverbs are *synonyms* expressing the same idea in different words, for instance, the notion that the world is full of women: "Woman is a chrysalis, no forest where it is not hanging" (Mongo, **I**. II, 15a), or "Women are like a duiker's dung" (Bemba, **I**. II, 15b). More rarely, proverbs are (almost) *homonyms* but, coming from different cultural contexts, they have different meanings, as in the case of: "A mother cannot die" (see for explanation **I**. V, 38a).

Proverbs are characterized by their conciseness. They are often in *telegraphic style*: words – especially articles, verbs, pronouns – are regularly omitted: "No words are wasted and all propositions are stated as succinctly as possible, with the common grammatical forms frequently curtailed and changed. The shortened forms especially provide many examples of rather archaic or cryptic speech" (Hamutyinei and Plangger 1974: 16). An example: "Family-name woman-wife: Yes. Don't go, I stay; don't speak, I am silent; don't do, I renounce" (Wolof; see for explanation **I**. III, 1).

It is obvious that a number of the most captivating features of proverbs are barely translatable – assonance, alliteration, rhyme, rhythm, and word play, to name just a few. The following proverb is a Yoruba example of word play: *Fọmú fọ́mọ, fọmọ fọ́mú; bí ọmọ bá ti mu ọmú, ko bù ṣe?* It means; "Give the breast to the baby, give the baby to the breast; as long as the baby sucks the breast, is that not the end of the matter? (Bamgbose, 1968: 84). The proverb plays on the contrast between *omu*, "breast", and *omo*, "child". Often part or most of the *jeu de mots* gets lost in the translation. Such losses are regrettable, but many proverbs stay vigorous and eloquent in spite of translation. And without, they would'not be accessible at all outside the original culture. (For a note on translation and text, see p.17.)

The use of *parallelism* (repetition with a difference) is frequent. Formal parallels in verbs, nouns or adjectives reinforce *similarities* and *contrasts* in meaning; e.g. "To bear a girl is to bear a problem" (Tigrinya, **I**. I, 1); "What the yam feels, the knife understands" (Yoruba, **I**. III, 26); "A mother lying down sees farther than a child on a tree" (Krio, **I**. V, 7).

Unconventional comparisons and surprising images underline the proverbs' deviation from ordinary speech. Thus, proverbially, woman can become a goat (Rwanda, **II**. X, 11), a mimosa tree (Xhosa, **I**. II, 11), a blanket (Ashanti, **I**. III, 13) or a used potato plot (Ganda, **II**. IV, 24).

Like the proverbs of other continents (cf. Roehrich, 1977: 60f), the proverbs of Africa exhibit regular patterns. Some main patterns are: (1) A is (like) B: e.g. "Woman is a goat, man a bright red cola nut" (Yaka, **I**. II, 19a); (2) A is unlike B: "Woman is not a corncob to be valued by stripping off its leaves" (Baule, **I**. II, 5b); (3) No A without B: "No woman without big sister" (Rwanda, **I**. II, 23); (4) Better A than B: "A stupid wife is better than a ruinous house" (Bassar, **I**. III, 10b); (5) If A then B: "If you dance with your co-wife, don't close your eyelid" (Rundi, **I**. IV, 15), or "If you are impatient to have a child, you marry a pregnant woman" (Fulani, **II**. IV, 20).

Proverbs are usually one sentence and seldom longer than two, as the given examples show. I shall now close these brief and, by necessity, incomplete remarks on some frequent features of proverbs. The ideas behind these characteristics are matters of ideology, content and use.

Silent and Invisible?

There might be serious objections to the interpretation of proverbs out of context, since they are said to come alive only in oral communication and to acquire new connotations each time they are quoted. Therefore, one could argue, it is difficult to attribute them, outside the live situation, with any definitive meaning. I certainly agree that a great deal of information is needed to analyze the full meaning and function and effect of each of the proverbs, information on origin, literal denotation and figurative sense; on users and addressees (gender, age group, position in society); on frequency of the proverb's use, acceptance and impact. And on their passing away. Information should also be gathered on counter-proverbs and parodies, and their potential neutralizing effects. This collection on women in proverbs is just a beginning and does not pretend to be more than a first step.

Nevertheless, some general remarks can be made on the present material. I have often asked African friends interested in proverbs on women whether they knew of similar negative proverbs used by women about men. They were unable to think of any, nor was I able to find any convincing example of such proverbs in the African collections I read (cf. the *Penguin Dictionary of Proverbs*: no section on "Man" at all, but a well-provided one on "Woman"). Not counting the numerous negative proverbs about women as such, most negative lessons and warnings in proverbs either include the whole of humanity or point to a very limited category of bad men, such as thieves or cheats. This does not prove that women are more sympathetic than men, nor does it mean that negative sayings about men do not exist among women, if they have not been described as yet. In my opinion, it does, however, make clear that:

(1) Women dare not (or are not allowed to) speak out as freely as men, as long as their roles are unequal to those of men in society (private versus public).
(2) Considerably more anthropological and sociological research has been done (in Africa and elsewhere) on men's than on women's views of society.

As far as the first point is concerned: in all unequal human relationships, the masters allow themselves to speak freely and openly about their subordinates. Being in power, they can afford to do so without any risk. Slaves, serfs, servants, colonized and other subjects, however, keep their thoughts and comments on their superiors to themselves, since they are scared of the repercussions such boldness might provoke. But among equals they do of course discuss in detail the masters' peculiarities, often without the superiors' awareness of the very existence of any such comments. Colonial Europeans, for example, generally did not know at all what Africans thought of them, communication on an equal footing being impossible in colonial relations. The example of the pot-lid criticism is an indication of gender relations among the Fiote. In this respect, many other proverbs throughout the book, especially on power-policy, are eloquent as well. The power position is often betrayed by the perspective. It seems hardly probable that anyone would pull to pieces the group he or she belongs to, and thus a negative statement carefully excludes one's own kind: "A woman is like a goat: she is tethered where the thistles grow" (Rwanda, **II**. X, 11). In a number of cases, the gender of the speaker can be detected from certain features of the proverb itself.

Another old question is, why – again, not only in Africa, but all over the world – proverbs and other derogatory statements about women should be so widespread. Could it be that fear and uncertainty, sublimated in domination, underlie the imposition of so many dictates and restrictions? Logically, if the situation were ideal and women were as humble as they should be, fear and uncertainty would be superfluous and no hostile proverbs would be needed about women. The ideal of the "Woman-wife whose name is Yes" is more a case of wishful thinking than a matter of fact. So, in reality, one may presume, women do resist, protest, refuse, flatter, manipulate, albeit indirectly. Not only proverbs but also other literary genres such as myth (cf. Schipper, 1985: 23–27) or poetry reveal how the dominant group, stuck on power, tries to maintain the status quo by means of language. In traditional Yoruba poetry, for example, women are singled out for attacks: Yoruba traditional poets, as Oyesakin (1985: 38) explained, reflect male-dominant society in blaming women for all the ills in society, and this has two inter-related aims:

> The first aim is to cajole women to succumb to the subservient role the society expects them to play. It is to curb the excesses of the spurious women so that they can conform to the societal norms. Secondly, the severe attack and condemnation of women in Yoruba traditional poetry aims at exposing women in such a way that men who invariably need them could exercise restraints at handling these "objects" they so much love and desire. In short, traditional poetry paints women as agents of indiscipline in the society.

Major bad qualities attributed to the Yoruba women in poetry are "loose tongue, avarice and lasciviousness" (ibid.). Female sexual immorality is especially emphasized, in poetry and in proverbs – and not only among the Yoruba. The Why?-question cannot really be answered without extensive research on gender relations as power relations.

As for the second point, ever since the rise of women's studies, the absence or "invisibility" of women in the study of history and society has often been noted. In *African Women: Their Struggle for Economic Independence* (1981:1), the Ugandan anthropologist

Christine Obbo stated that "nearly half the people of most societies have not been allowed the chance or space to articulate their thoughts, fears, and hopes on the subjects of labour, reproduction, child-bearing and sexuality". According to her, the roles of women have often been either trivialized or considered less relevant by scholars, and the result has been that the different realities and viewpoints of various segments of society were dealt with inadequately. Obbo admits that, due to traditions, African women have perhaps been less accessible than men to predominantly male researchers, but she denounces most researchers' automatic assumption "that men are better informants because they seem involved in the crucial cultural activities" (*ibid.*: 3). Her study on women's rural-urban migration reveals that women "who had never heard of any Women's Movement in the West, questioned male supremacy in all aspects of life as well as the associated myths of the inevitability of marriage, the undesirability of illegitimate children and the general problem of the way women's place is assumed to be subordinate and dependent upon men as fathers, brothers and husbands" (p. 4). Through migration, hard work and manipulation, women created strategies for achieving economic independence and better social conditions. They did so in spite of their men's obvious need to control women, which "has always been an important part of male success in most African societies". The women wanted to change the traditional ideologies in their own way. Obbo's remark on research in the humanities confirms our second statement. She also illustrates our first statement – on women's secrecy due to their subordinate position – when she notes that Ugandan women's strategies "were known to all [women] but were disseminated discreetly in private conversation or as knowledge stored up from childhood observations of female relatives. Although most village women took care not to let the children know their strategies by speaking in riddles, such caution would be forgotten in moments of stress" (*ibid.*: 4f). As a result of research like Obbo's, women's lives do indeed become more visible.

"The Words of Women Do Not Fall Down"

In recent years, more general information has rapidly become available on the role of women in African society (e.g. Barbier, 1985; Cutrufelli, 1983; Oppong, 1983). Despite persistent efforts, however, I found only one article on the subject of women and proverbs: Amba Oduyoye's indignant "The Asante woman: socialization through proverbs" (1979). She studied the crucial impact of proverbial imagery about women in society to "elicit the realistic situation of women in Asante", convinced as she was that language about women, in particular proverbs, influences sex role socialization. Proverbs reinforce women's images and justify the roles ascribed to girls, wives, mothers, widows and so forth. Their picture presented in proverbs is used to legitimize the roles and functions of women. Her inside observations on Ashanti women seem quite relevant to a number of the proverbs in this collection: "those women who do not fit the composite picture are marginalized by their own social group, other women, as well as by men. Thus one encounters such generalized statements as: women cannot keep a secret, they demand impossible feats from men, they prove to be unfaithful . . . Yet the fact remains that it is a composite picture which mediates against the individual woman to be a person" (Oduyoye, 1979: 5).

The same article mentioned some proverbs that, thanks to their emphasis on the individual's value irrespective of sex and status, could be used to counteract the numerous anti-female quotes. For example, "All people are the children of God", or "We are all children of eggs – we come from the same source"; but these are "few and far between" (*ibid.*: 5, 6).

In our collection, many African proverbs emphasize the reproductive function of women as their main aspect: "Girl, bring forth, that we may see what you're worth" (Bembe, **I**. I, 4). The polygamous inclination of men is presented as quite natural, whereas women's interest in other men becomes unfaithfulness. A woman needs to pay deference to a man, because she "stays in womanhood" (or childhood, which is the same) according to a Gikuyu proverb (**II**. X, 4). Women's behaviour has often been patterned by such thinking. The strategy seems to declare a number of jobs difficult and therefore a man's business, and women are not allowed to assume male roles. If they do, it is useless anyway, because "the glory will go to a male", in Oduyoye's words. She quotes an eloquent proverb on the matter: "When a woman makes the giant drum, it is kept in the man's room" (Ashanti, **II**. VI, 34).

Marriage is an absolute social must, as many proverbs state. However, if one compares the social consequences of this male– female relationship, one has to conclude that men are obviously better off than women. This is noted in proverbs expressing male contempt for domestic chores such as fetching water, cooking or cleaning. Again, the perspective is clear: "A bad home sends you for water and fire wood" (Rwanda, **II**. VI, 13a), warning a man not to let his wife dominate him, or he'll end up drawing water, cooking and so forth, and that is woman's work.

Fertility and motherhood are women's most important qualities, but the sterile woman and the widow are quite pitiful, according to a number of proverbs. Women are objects of fear and distrust: even after a long marriage a man should remember that they always remain "outsiders" in "your" home.

Sometimes solidarity among women is expressed and sometimes women's rivalry or their complicity with the system. The most loving relationship is the one between mothers and children, whereas the one between husbands and wives is fraught with problems. One has no choice, unfortunately: "Lacking a mother, one takes a wife" (Hausa, **I**. III, 8).

In conclusion, the proverbial image-building has been strong and the male–female relations are presented as natural and unquestioned. "The bearded mouth does not lie" (Bemba, Zambia) and "The words of men do not fall down" (Shona, Zimbabwe). The Akan women's saying "I won't come back female" (in another life, that is) expresses the unbelief in change during one's life time, but it also emphasizes dissatisfaction: "If women indeed constitute the majority of witches one could interpret that fact as a form of protest against their factual powerlessness in society". (Oduyoye, 1979: 12). None the less, it is likely that women have often willingly accepted their unequal position and made the best of it, in the first place from sheer impotence, but probably also because they did not so much associate their rights with those of men. As long as the male and the female domains are accepted as "naturally" hierarchical and sepa-rate, women are perhaps more inclined to compare their situation with that of other women, their mothers, sisters, co-wives and friends. Today, especially in the urban areas, women do compare their social position and personal rights with those of men. More often than before they claim the same freedom, jobs and opportuni-ties. They want their share in public life and no longer put up with their role in the private sphere.

And what will happen to the proverbs, "cream of language" and "horses of speech"? For the purpose of new model-building, it might be interesting to replace in proverbs the negative by the positive, the word woman female by the word man/male and vice versa, not as a solution but as an exercise, to see what it looks like from the other side. Where old proverbs lose their relevance, they will be forgotten, but wherever the need for new ones is strongly felt, they will certainly be created. As the Ganda put it: "An old proverb authorizes a new one."

NOTE ON TRANSLATION
AND PRESENTATION

If no English translation has been furnished by other sources, all the proverbs in this book are presented in as literal a translation as possible. Whenever necessary, a short comment has been added. If the comment is a quotation, it is marked as such. All the oral and written sources and references can be found at the back of the book. If a proverb has been provided by more than one source, both references are given. In a number of cases, two or more proverbs figure as a, b, c under the same number, as synonyms or as variants with slightly different wordings. The languages and countries have been put in brackets; sometimes, for the sake of clarity, a word has been added inside the proverb and such words are within square brackets.

PART ONE

PHASES OF LIFE

I

GIRL

1. To bear a girl is to bear a problem. (*Tigrinya, Ethiopia*)

2. A nice navel does not prevent a girl from suffering. (*Rundi, Burundi*)

   = In spite of her beauty a girl can be unhappy.

3. When the dance is in full swing, the girl's upper legs can be seen. (*Baule, Côte d'Ivoire*)

   = Her loin-cloth may swirl up during the dance: if you put all your energy in your work, the result will be admired.

4. Girl, bring forth, that we may see what you're worth. (*Bembe, Zaïre*)

5. The milk of a girl is in her sex. (*Rwanda, Rwanda*)

   = "Milk and cows are a symbol of prosperity. If a girl does not find a husband to have children with, she will be miserable."

6. No cocksure girl has beaten the skin skirt. (*Ndebele, Zimbabwe; Zulu, South Africa*)

   = "Marriage will tame the wild or cocksure woman. When a woman got married in olden days, she wore the skin skirt to show she was married."

7. A girl flutters her breasts without knowing the consequences. (*Rwanda, Rwanda*)

   = "A girl imagines she'll always stay young." The proverb is a warning, reminding one to think of the future.

8. No girl holds herself in contempt. (*Rwanda, Rwanda; Swahili, East Africa*)

   = "Every girl imagines she pleases."

9. What a girl wants, she'll get at any price. (*Rwanda, Rwanda*)

10. One girl misbehaves, all are insulted. (*Rwanda, Rwanda*)

11. A maiden does not collect wet fuel. (*Zulu, South Africa/ Swaziland; Ndebele, Zimbabwe*)

   = "Wet fuel does not burn easily and, therefore, it is not collected. Only dry wood is collected. A girl will always have some man attracted by her". No girl needs to stay unmarried.

12. When the figs are ripe, all the birds want them. (*Mandinka, Guinea*)

   = "A nubile girl is an object of covetousness."

13. Brought up among boys, the young girl weakens. (*Gikuyu, Kenya*)

   = "The boys eat faster and more, so the girl is undernourished." The weak ones cannot compete with the strong ones.

14. A favourite girl is not to be trusted. (*Ganda, Uganda*)

   = "A tree may look straight and nice, but the wood might be useless. Appearances are deceptive."

15. She shows respect even where she has no lover. (*Ndebele, Zimbabwe*)

   = "A girl should respect everyone she meets (not just relatives), as anyone may in future turn out to be a member of the family she marries into."

16. When fate gives the sign, a girl makes love to the guest. (*Rwanda, Rwanda*)

   = "Transgression of an interdict is the portent of misfortune."

17. In front of something frightening, girls sit down decently. (*Rundi, Burundi*)

   = In case of difficulties one has to think before acting.

18. The day of her excision, no water in the well. (*Minyanka, Mali*)

= After the excision, there is always the risk of haemorrhage and one needs water to wash the wound. The excision itself is already a bad experience; if the lack of water adds up to this, it means bad luck.
> Bad luck always finds the unfortunate.

19. Even the ugly girl must suffer excision. (*Minyanka, Mali*)

= "All girls [among the Minyanka] have to undergo clitoridectomy before marriage."
> No exception to the rule. Everybody is in the same position.

20. An unmarried girl is like a bushbuck: one who will not spear it, stalks it. (*Ganda, Uganda*)

= "A desirable girl has many suitors."

21. The hunchback is married off to her neighbours. (*Zulu, South Africa/Swaziland*)

= "If a girl has some defect, physical or otherwise, it is best if she marries people who know her well and are more likely to tolerate her."

22. Girls do not know the troubles of wives. (*Minyanka, Mali*)

= "Before their excision, girls live happily; they have no responsibilities, no troubles, no household problems. They dance and play in between cooking times. Nevertheless they yearn for marriage which will make them 'adult'."
> "If I do not have your difficulties, I have others as serious ones. E.g. the city woman coming back to the village on a visit to her friends is told that she must be lucky to live in the city: no water to carry, no flour to grind, money to buy things and so on. The woman quotes the proverb."

23. A pregnant girl is not married for the first kitchen. (*Namibia*)

= "By allowing herself to be made pregnant, she has forfeited the chance of becoming a chief's first wife."

24. Better "little woman" than "little girl". (*Rwanda, Rwanda*)

= "The fate of a girl is worse than that of a woman. Of two evils choose the lesser."

25. (a) A girl is a peanut seed: she enlarges the clan. (*Woyo, Zaïre*)
(b) A clan with female posterity cannot perish. (*Kongo, Zaïre*)

= "The clan prospers as long as there are nubile girls."

II

WOMAN

1. (a) Woman is like the earth: everyone sits down on her. (*Lingala, Zaïre*)
    (b) Woman is like the earth: even a fool sits down on her. (*Lulua, Zaïre*)

2. Woman without man is a field without seed. (*Luba, Zaïre*)

3. A woman's rope is ready on the porch. (*Ganda, Uganda*)

    = "A woman offended by her husband is soon ready to say: 'I am going to hang myself.' "

4. Women and sky cannot be understood. (*Gikuyu, Kenya*)

5. (a) Woman is not cassava to be valued by roasting and tasting. (*Baule, Ivory Coast*)
    (b) Woman is not a corncob to be valued by stripping off its leaves. (*Baule, Ivory Coast*)

    = "Woman is a mysterious being, difficult to know. Only long experience will teach you whether the woman you married is the wife who suits you."

6. (a) Woman, remember that the mouth is sometimes covered with a branch. (*Gikuyu, Kenya*)
    (b) No secrets before a woman. (*Shona, Zimbabwe*)

    = "Women generally fail to keep secrets."

7. The owl says: "Who gossips with the women is a woman." (*Fulani, Cameroon/Nigeria/Chad*)

24

8. Calumny spoken at the well is heard by the frog. (*Sena, Malawi/ Mozambique*)

   = "Never speak a secret in the public place where women draw water."

9. Who will not marry a talkative woman stays a bachelor. (*Mongo, Zaïre*)

10. Woman is fire. If you have to, take a little. (*Fulani, Senegal*)

    = "To make fire, the housewife usually goes to a neighbour to ask for some live coals, which she takes home on a potsherd. She picks them up by hand from the neighbour's fire and so takes tiny bits at a time. One must practise the same caution towards women, dangerous creatures."

11. A woman is like the mimosa tree that yields gum all day long. (*Xhosa, South Africa*)

    = The image "arises from the Xhosa fondness for chewing gum": she makes you profit all the time.

12. Woman is like a shadow: go to her, she flees; leave her, she follows you. (*Luba, Zaïre; Somali, Somalia*)

13. Women are like gourds: they cannot balance. (*Gikuyu, Kenya*)

    = "Women are unstable."

14. Woman is like the milk of a young coconut, unpleasing except in its shell. (*Swahili, East Africa*)

    = "Said of the shyness of women on a visit, away from their own home."

15. (a) Woman is a chrysalis: there is no forest where it is not hanging. (*Mongo, Zaïre*)
    (b) Women are like a duiker's dung. (*Bemba, Zambia*)

    = "Women are as plentiful as duikers' dung; so if your wife misbehaves, throw her out and find another one."

16. A woman is like a shield: you call it light until you try it on. (*Ganda, Uganda*)

17. A woman is like the unpeeled bark of a tree: whoever draws near may peel it off. (*Shona, Zimbabwe*)

    = "Things owned in common usually do not last long, since anyone can come and use them as he wishes, just as anyone can go and propose to an unmarried woman who belongs to no one in particular."

18. Woman is like a winnowing basket; wherever it goes, it winnows. (*Fulani, Senegal*)

= "Wherever she goes. a woman is always only a woman."

19. (a) Woman is a goat, man a bright red cola nut. (*Yaka, Zaïre*)

= "Women are naïve and weak, men are clever and strong."

(b) Woman sees the rain, man sees the spider. (*Yaka, Zaïre*)

= "Man sees the spider and his web, sign of morning fog or of drizzly rain coming. He warns his wife, who does not listen to him. He himself is not taken by surprise."

20. A woman is a basket of flour; the hungry come of their own accord. (*Umbundu, Angola*)

21. Women are like earthenware plates: not to be thrown in the waste pit. (*Kongo, Zaïre*)

= "Women have to be respected."

22. A woman is more than her breasts; goats also have two. (*Rwanda, Rwanda*)

= "It is not enough for a woman to belong to the female sex; she must also have some qualities."

23. No woman without big sister. (*Rwanda, Rwanda*)

= "No wise person does not find someone wiser than her/himself."

24. For woman, display is dishonour. (*Swahili, Tanzania*)

25. Let a female develop her breast; one day, she must give it to her child. (*Igbo, Nigeria*)

= "Remember that a female should act like a female."

26. Breast-ache is not man's ache. (*Minyanka, Mali*)

= "Can be quoted in all cases where the gender division of work is not respected: a man who prepares a sauce, a woman who makes a field ready for sowing, a girl on a bicycle, a boy spinning cotton, and so on."

27. If a woman praises you for climbing a tree, she is praising you for falling. (*Mamprusi, Burkina Faso*)

= "If you believe in flattery, you will have an accident."

28. A rich woman's bracelet is not too big for her arm. (*Bassar, Togo*)

= "Quoted when somebody criticizes you because of your fortune."

29. A woman who admits guilt will not spend time on her knees. (*Yoruba, Nigeria; Hausa, Niger/Nigeria*)

= "He who admits his faults will prosper."

30. One who seeks a wife does not speak contemptuously of women. (*Ashanti, Ghana*)

I I I

WIFE

1. The family name of the woman-wife is Yes. You say: "Don't
   go;" she says: "I stay." You say: "Don't speak;" she says: "I
   am silent." You say: "Don't do;" she says: "I renounce."
   (*Wolof, Senegal*)

2. No wife, no trouble yet. (*Mamprusi, Burkina Faso*)

   = "If you avoid responsibility, you also avoid trouble."

3. If you haven't seen the bride, don't unroll the sleeping mat.
   (*Mandinka, Senegal*)

   = "Before the bride comes to her new domicile, her hut is made ready for her,
   including a mat. However, it happens that the newly married woman flees
   before the marriage rituals have been accomplished." In general: Wait and
   see how things develop before taking new steps.

4. Do not show the old field to the new wife. (*Mandinka, Guinea*)

   = "It is not wise to expose your miseries as soon as your young bride enters
   your house."

5. A man's ear is like a nubile woman. (*Mamprusi, Burkina Faso*)

   = "A young woman as a new wife brings change, novelty and enjoyment to a
   man. The ear also enables a man to discover something new every day.
   Openness to change and novelty is a source of renewed enjoyment."

6. Even a basket of leaves frightens the young wife. (*Bassar, Togo*)

   = "If you are not courageous, anything can make you flee, be it wearisome
   work or responsibility."

Wife

7. The stupid husband lends his lance to his wife. (*Rundi, Burundi*)

= "It is best to keep any dangerous objects away from them."

8. Lacking a mother, one takes a wife. (*Hausa, Nigeria*)

= "A mother is more useful and less trouble."

9. Wives are without importance. (*Shilluk, Sudan*)

10. (a) Better a bad wife than an empty house. (*Baule, Ivory Coast*)
(b) A stupid wife is better than a ruinous house. (*Bassar, Togo*)

= Is a reply to those who criticize you. Often used as an argument in a palaver.

11. The man may be the head of the home; the wife is the heart. (*Gikuyu, Kenya*)

12. A man without a pitcher is always thirsty. (*Yaka, Zaïre*)

= "A man without wife yearns for one because, truly, she soothes all needs."

13. A wife is like a blanket: cover yourself, it irritates you; cast it aside, you feel the cold. (*Ashanti, Ghana*)

14. The wife of the rich man lacked a ring. (*Tonga, Zambia*)

= "Nobody can have everything in life."

15. Pluck the pumpkin, you must take the leaves. (*Tonga, Zambia*)

= "A man must take care of not only his wife but his wife's relatives as well, for by marriage he has contracted a certain obligation towards them all."

16. If you want peace, give ear to your wife's proposals. (*Fang, Cameroon/Equatorial Guinea/Gabon*)

17. There is some remedy for a fool who will listen, but there is no medicine for a bad wife who will not take good counsel. (*Somali, Somalia*)

18. Wives and oxen have no friends. (*Gikuyu, Kenya*)

= One cannot show kindness to the extent of giving away one's wife or one's ox.

19. A wife is like an old cooking-pot: you don't let your friend keep it for you. (*Ganda, Uganda*)

= Take care of it yourself, because "it might be spoiled".

20. A wife is not meat to be parcelled up and sent out to others. (*Ashanti, Ghana*)

21. In a good marriage you bring his food without having to dress up for it. (*Ganda, Uganda*)

= "An exacting husband would quarrel."

22. If the marriage has lasted for a long time, you'll have to ask your wife for a roasted banana. (*Ganda, Uganda*)

= "In the beginning you were given it without asking – love has cooled down."

23. The wife of a fearless husband can only be taken away when he is not at home. (*Ganda, Uganda*)

24. (a) The belly precedes the child. (*Rundi, Burundi*)

= "Refers to women who prefer a man to her child."

(b) The favourite wife of the grasshopper will carry her husband, but not her child. (*Rundi, Burundi*)

=Same as (a), but also quoted to mock flatterers.

25. Now the marriage is going to begin, as the neglected wife said when she was flogged with thorns. (*Hausa, Niger/Nigeria*)

= "Even ill treatment is better than utter neglect."

26. What the yam feels, the knife understands. (*Yoruba, Nigeria*)

= "Just as the knife is the closest thing to the yam, so the husband is the closest person to the wife. He alone fully understands her." Applied as a comment on close human relationships.

27. A woman is wife only through her husband. (*Rundi, Burundi*)

= "Nothing can be realized without others. Expresses solidarity and the fact that people need each other to complete themselves."

28. A man changing his abode is like a woman marrying. (*Gikuyu, Kenya*)

= "As a woman, on marrying, adopts the customs of the family she enters, so a man going to live in a strange country must accept its customs."

29. Little by little the stranger's shit comes nearer to the village. (*Minyanka, Mali*)

= "The stranger is the new bride, just arrived in the village. Normally the women go out in the evening, together or separately, to relieve themselves in the surroundings of the village. A newly arrived woman feels embarrassed to do this, because she was not born there. Quoted for instance when a child, little by little, makes progress in school. The proverb is said to encourage him: everything will be fine in the end."

30. They marry a wife because of the child. (*Mamprusi, Burkina Faso*)

= "Dependence is accepted for the sake of gain."

31. If a wife has left her husband, and the milk is curdling, she won't be long in coming back. (*Fulani, Senegal*)

= "When the husband is rich, it will not be difficult for him to get his wife back."

32. She who says: "Oh, Misery!" will die in her married state; she who says: "I cannot bear it" will leave. (*Ganda, Uganda*)

33. (a) Your wife may flee you, but she does not die. (*Ganda, Uganda*)

= "As long as he considers her as his wife, he is her husband. After her death he is called 'widower'."

(b) Your woman runs away, but she does not defame you. (*Ganda, Uganda*)

= "In Buganda it would be a breach of the accepted code."

34. A woman who has not been married twice cannot know perfect marriage. (*Yoruba, Nigeria*)

35. Women are of two kinds: those who enrich you, those who impoverish you. (*Fulani, Senegal*)

= "There is the good housewife, serious and saving; there is the wasteful and careless wife who ruins her husband if he does not set his house in order."

36. A toadstool needs only one leg to stand on. (*Fiote, Cabinda*)

= Message offered by a wife to her husband through a pot-lid,[*] meaning: "I have one husband, you, and that is enough for me." The pot-lid with a toadstool on it is a sign of the wife's fidelity in marriage.

---

[*] For explanation of the proverbial pot-lid messages, see Introduction, p. 9.

37. One pestle needs only one mortar to pound. (*Vili, Cabinda*)

= Message sculpted in images on a pot-lid* (covering food) offered to a husband to express his wife's protest against his intention to take a second wife.

38. I have a pot, why search for another? (*Kru, Liberia*)

= On being content with oneself, especially referring to monogamous marriage.

39. (a) No man is a hero to his wife. (*Swahili, East Africa*)
(b) The wife does not call her husband hero. (*Mongo, Zaïre*)
(c) The woman has no king. (*Ndebele, Zimbabwe*)

= She "does not respect or fear her husband's position."

(d) Women have no king. (*Bari, Sudan*)

= Two explanations: (i) "By sticking together they always get their will done." (ii) "Women are more radical than men. They act without restraint." > Impossible to control them.

---

* For explanation of the proverbial pot-lid messages, see Introduction, p. 9.

I V

CO-WIFE

1. The feet of the first wife do not walk in the dew of the morning grass. (*Fang, Cameroon/Gabon*)

   = The first wife has some privileges: she sleeps a little later than the other wives.

2. You, first wife, speak; you, second, be silent. (*Yaka, Zaïre*)

   = The first wife is held in greater respect than the second one.

3. A woman's value is not her being the first wife. (*Mongo, Zaïre*)

   = "Her value depends on the love for her husband, her behaviour, her zest for work, and so on."

4. The favoured wife does not grow fat. (*Kundu, Cameroon*)

   = "In order to keep her position, she must work very hard, and the other wives, jealous, nag her continuously."

5. The first wife is like a mother. (*Swahili, East Africa*)

   = "Used by polygamist to justify a second wife; refers also to the vital part first wives play in running homes."

6. The first wife is like magic: you never get rid of her. (*Mongo, Zaïre*)

7. The rod that is used to beat the senior wife is waiting in the roof for the junior. (*Yoruba, Nigeria; Mamprusi, Burkina Faso; Krio, Sierra Leone*)

   = Juniors will suffer in the same way their seniors have suffered.

8. If a wife sees the stick that beats her co-wife, she throws it into the wilds. (*Ganda, Uganda*)

9. The first one makes the home. (*Tonga, Zambia*)

= "A warning to those married to more than one woman. They should not despise the first wife. She is the one who knows them so well. When the day of trouble comes, it will be she who looks after them and supports them. The other(s) will not do so, even though they may be loved so much."

10. The new cooking-pot never scorns the old one. (*Minyanka, Mali*)

= "A young wife must respect the first wife who is older than she is."

11. The new wife does not know that the first one is loved. (*Baatonum, Benin*)

12. If you have a new earthen pot, don't throw away the old one. (*Swahili, Zaïre; Ngwana, Zaïre*)

13. When the favourite wife commits a fault, the despised one rejoices. (*Ganda, Uganda*)

= "Malicious joy at another person's misfortune."

14. The stone on the ground, the foot walking: they'll always clash. (*Mandinka, Senegal*)

= "Co-wives always fight."

15. If you dance with your co-wife, don't close your eyelid. (*Rundi, Burundi*)

= She'll try to trip you up.

16. The mouse cuts the broom in the hut; the wife and her rival will accuse each other. (*Mamprusi, Burkina Faso*)

= "The smallest excuse is enough for enemies to accuse each other."

17. If a wife has kicked her co-wife, it is on the husband's shoulder she has found support. (*Fulani, Senegal*)

= "A wife would never dare beat her co-wife if she were not sure to be the preferred one of the husband."

18. You measure some flour for your co-wife and this flour makes your husband spend the night with her. (*Rundi, Burundi*)

= "The polygamous husband stays with the wife who receives him best." In other words, you help her, but she profits at your cost.

19. You scorn the small vulva of your co-wife, but it takes away your husband. (*Rwanda, Rwanda*)

20. A wife cannot quarrel with her husband without mentioning her co-wife. (*Mongo, Zaïre*)

21. A palaver with a co-wife, the indemnification is a child. (*Mongo, Zaïre*)

= A mother's warning to her daughters. "Don't quarrel with your co-wife: you pay the highest price." She might revenge herself on one of your children.

22. The foolish wife imagines her co-wife has taken care. (*Rwanda, Rwanda*)

= You can never trust your co-wife.

23. A rival begets an avenger. (*Rwanda, Rwanda*)

24. A man with one wife is chief among the unmarried. (*Ganda, Uganda*)

= In the kingdom of the blind, the one-eyed man is king.

25. A man whose only wife falls ill, gets thin. (*Ganda, Uganda*)

= "All the work is on him and nobody cooks for him. Therefore it is better to have several wives."

26. Only one wife, only one jar in one's basket. (*Yaka, Zaïre*)

27. To have one wife is to be one-eyed. (*Luba, Zaïre*)

28. If you marry two, you'll die all the younger. (*Luba, Zaïre*)

29. Two wives, two pots of poison. (*Gikuyu, Kenya*)

30. A man who married many wives can stay hungry. (*Gikuyu, Kenya*)

= A glutton is never satisfied.

Source of all Evil

31. A thousand wives, a thousand palavers. (*Ashanti, Ghana*)

32. Hypocrisy is a woman with both husband and co-wife on her back. (*Fulani, Niger/Nigeria*)

33. Beat the bad wife with a new wife. (*Nobiin, Sudan*)

= "Marry another one."

V

MOTHER

1. Mother is gold, father is mirror. (*Yoruba, Nigeria*)

   = "A mirror is fragile and unreliable because it may break at any time. Gold is solid and stable – just as the mother is, closer to the child than the father is expected to be."

2. A wife should be like one's mother. (*Swahili, Tanzania*)

3. A mother of twins does not lie on her side. (*Mano, Liberia; Fulani/Wolof, Senegal*)

   = "She has to nurse the two equally and at the same time."

4. A mother's tears are no work. (*Mongo, Zaïre*)

   = "Love does not know fatigue, shame etc."

5. The child's mother grabs the sharp end of the knife. (*Tswana, South Africa/Botswana; Sotho, Lesotho*)

   = She'll take any risk to protect her child.

6. The mother declares she is lying down, but her feet are outside. (*Baule, Ivory Coast*).

   = "She is never quiet, always preoccupied with what might happen to her children."

7. A mother lying down sees farther than a child on a tree. (*Krio, Sierra Leone*)

8. (a) Mother is God number two. (*Chewa, Malawi*)
(b) A mother is not bought. (*Ganda, Uganda*)

= "A good mother is a gift of God." One cannot buy her.

9. A cow never runs away from her calves. (*Bemba, Zambia*)

10. A mother-mouse does not make her own stomach sweet. (*Tonga, Zambia*)

= "A parent, especially the mother, always thinks of the child, to the extent of forgetting herself so much that even the tiniest bit she is given she always thinks of sharing it with her child. She cannot have her stomach really satisfied."

11. The panther does not fear the stains on its mother's skin. (*Mandinka, Senegal*)

= A child is not afraid of its mother even though she may be wicked to others.

12. The baby who refuses its mother's breast will never be fully grown. (*Gikuyu, Kenya*)

= "You can only develop with the proper nourishment."

13. A fool will suck his dead mother. (*Gikuyu, Kenya*)

= "He is far from wise who tries to derive benefit where none can be."

14. If your mother is not there, your bowels ache while eating. (*Ganda, Uganda*)

= "The presence of the mother sweetens the food."

15. A mother suckles, even on the road. (*Rundi, Burundi*)

16. Pity comes to a mother when she sees that the food is ending. (*Ganda, Uganda*)

17. A mother of many children has no *ggobe* left. (*Ganda, Uganda*)

= *Ggobe* are the leaves of beans. "A mother gives everything for her children."

18. When your mother dies, you'll eat yam peels. (*Ngbaka, Central African Republic*)

19. Food for the child gives the mother a small belly. (*Rwanda, Rwanda*)

= "The mother profits from gifts people bring to her new-born child."

20. The child who has a mother does not drivel. (*Rwanda, Rwanda*)

= Is not neglected.

21. An insolent child has only a mother. (*Ganda, Uganda*)

= "The father would punish it."

22. The child has eaten the partridge; his mother vomits feathers. (*Rundi, Burundi*)

= "Parents are responsible for the faults of their children."

23. (a) A bad child brings shame upon the mother. (*Ganda, Uganda*)

(b) It is not the mother's will to have a bad offspring. (*Gikuyu, Kenya*)

24. (a) One's ivory ring never gets too heavy to carry. (*Tonga, Zambia*)
(b) An elephant never tires of carrying his tusks. (*Vai, Liberia; Chewa, Malawi; Shona, Zimbabwe*)

= "One's children can never be too much of a burden to care for."

25. The mother of an ugly child keeps it on her back. (*Ganda, Uganda*)

= "She is shy of showing it to people."

26. A child acquires habits when still in the *ngozi*. (*Ganda, Uganda*)

= The *ngozi* is the cloth for carrying the child on the back of the mother.

27. A mother with no relatives must dance with the child on her back. (*Kundu, Cameroon*)

= "If you have no helpers you are miserable."

28. The child who bites the back of his mother will find no other willing to carry him. (*Yoruba, Nigeria*)

29. A child that does not cry will die on his mother's back. (*Zulu, South Africa*)

= "Please, say what you have to say."

30. The mother of the beautiful one has no ears. (*Gikuyu, Kenya*)

= Don't be influenced by other people's flattery.

31. The pillow your mother snores on wants for nothing. (*Rundi, Burundi*)

= "The mother intercedes for the children with the father and uses her bed secrets to attain her object."

32. With money, no mother. (*Gikuyu, Kenya*)

= "In business one should be strict and show no favour."

33 (a) The breast of your mother is not to be forgotten. (*Tonga, Zambia*)
(b) A mother's breast cannot be abandoned because of a wound. (*Mboshi, Congo*)

= "Take care of your mother who cared for you when you were young. Do not forget her and the trouble she took bringing you up." In general: you must take care of older relatives who took care of you as a child.

34. He who takes anything to his mother never says it is too heavy. (*Ganda, Uganda*)

= "For one's mother no sacrifice is too big."

35. Your mother is still your mother, though her legs be small. (*Chewa, Malawi*)

= "Respect your parents even if they are lame and you are much better off than them."

36. (a) An old hare is suckled by her young. (*Ganda, Uganda*)
(b) The hide that served the mother to carry the child will serve the child to carry the mother. (*Mboshi, Congo*)

= "What the mother has done for the children, the children must do for their parents."

37. No one entrusts his mother to drunks. (*Rundi, Burundi*)

= "One does not expose to danger those to whom one is attached."

38. (a) A mother cannot die. (Mongo, Zaïre)

= "She ought to be immortal. It is a sort of wish. A man would prefer never to be separated from his mother. If it would depend on him she would never die."

(b) A mother does not die. (*Ganda, Uganda*)

= "Her children keep on praising her."

39. The mother has died. Now for the good times. (*Kundu, Cameroon*)

= "Many hope life will be better for them when they have become independent."

40. It is not only one mother who can cook a nice soup. (*Efik, Nigeria; Ga, Ghana*)

41. (a) A son who never leaves home always thinks his mother's is the loudest fart. (*Gikuyu, Kenya*)
(b) A man does not die where his mother is. (*Mongo, Zaïre*)

= "He must dare undertake all kinds of things, travel, not be afraid of war and so on."

42. One without a mother should never get a sore on his back. (*Yoruba, Nigeria*)

= "A person cannot reach a sore on his own back, so when he gets one, his mother usually treats it for him. However, if his mother is dead, he would be well advised to avoid getting one. The proverb cautions against foolish behaviour."

43. One hundred aunts are not equal to one mother. (*Krio, Sierra Leone*)

44. (a) One mother comforts the other. (*Rwanda, Rwanda*)
(b) One mother never ridicules the other. (*Rundi, Burundi*)

V I

DAUGHTER

1. A new daughter is many voices. (*Gikuyu, Kenya*)

    = Everyone is interested in and comments upon the new and attractive.

2. (a) A daughter is like a raindrop: she'll fecundate others' fields. (*Luba, Zaïre*)
    (b) A girl-child is like a *mutuba*: those who profit did not plant. (*Ganda, Uganda*)

    = The *mutuba* is the fig tree. "Parents [fathers] often die before the girl gets married. Others receive the dowry."

3. The good daughter passes the poor man's gate. (*Gikuyu, Kenya*)

    = "Anything good has to be forfeited when one has no means of getting it."

4. The daughter is a mat for the guests. (*Rundi, Burundi*)

    = She must serve and satisfy her parents' visitors.

5. A daughter is not a guest. (*Rwanda, Rwanda*)

    = "She is naturally subservient."

6. A daughter is not a fisherman's net to be placed in all brooks. (*Kongo, Zaïre*)

    = "A daughter deserves respect and should not be yielded to the very first man you meet."

7. A father wants a huge dowry; his daughters grow old without husbands. (*Rwanda, Rwanda*)

8. None is abused for having a daughter as long as he can still bring forth. (*Rwanda, Rwanda*)

= There is still hope: the next child can be a son.

9. Who brings forth a daughter also gets a son. (*Ganda, Uganda*)

= When she marries.

10. The bellowing one gives birth to the lowing one. (*Rwanda, Rwanda*)

= "The daughter takes after the mother."

11. What itches in the woman's cloth itches in the girl's. (*Rwanda, Rwanda*)

= "One cannot blame others for faults one has oneself. For instance: a woman catches her daughter in the very act of making love and starts rebuking her; the daughter answers by the proverb."

12. A woman's eldest daughter is the one who takes her place. (*Rwanda, Rwanda*)

= After her death.

13. The mother of a daughter never lacks salt in the house. (*Rwanda, Rwanda*)

= "Daughters are provident by nature."

14. A mother of only daughters does not laugh before the others. (*Rwanda, Rwanda*)

= She is less respected than the mother of sons.

15. No daughter can vie with her mother. (*Rwanda, Rwanda*)

= "The effect is never superior to the cause."

16. Who can love me but hate my mother? (*Kundu, Cameroon*)

= "A man is fighting with his wife and tries to flatter his daughter. However, she turns away from him quoting the proverb."
> Solidarity daughter–mother.

VII

MOTHER-IN-LAW

1. Do not laugh at your mother-in-law for you will get a sty in your eye. (*Swahili, East Africa*)

2. Your mother-in-law does not serve you cooked corn but she engages you to grind. (*Rundi, Burundi*)

= You are not her guest but her servant.

3. To be accepted by your mother-in-law means less than to be loved by her daughter. (*Fulani, Cameroon/Chad/Nigeria*)

4. A mother-in-law is a *phuumbu* yam; the earth favours her. (*Yaka, Zaïre*)

= "A woman who visits her married daughter prospers like this yam which grows very big: she receives meat and palm-wine from her son-in-law."

5. Don't mock a thin mother-in-law. (*Ewe, Togo*)

6. If you have pulled down your mother-in-law, press! God knows when you will have another chance. (*Fulani, Senegal*)

= "If you can harm your mother-in-law, do not spare her. You very rarely have the chance to do so."

7. If you get along with your mother-in-law but not with your father-in-law, you have forgotten your being son-in-law. (*Minyanka, Mali*)

= Both parents-in-law can make life impossible. Therefore, take care of your own affairs, do not rely on your in-laws.

8. Your mother-in-law digs you a trap and God prepares you an issue. (*Rundi, Burundi*)

= Against your enemies, try and find strong helpers.

9. The mother-in-law shows you her buttocks without shame; the shame is yours. (*Bembe, Zaïre*)

= When women publicly show their bottom to a man, as a sign of protest against male behaviour, it is meant and felt as a deeply insulting gesture in a number of African societies.

10. Better the glares of a foreigner than those of a mother-in-law. (*Rundi, Burundi*)

= "One suffers more from one's relatives' hatred than from foreigners' negative feelings."

11. "Thank God" is better than thanking your mother-in-law. (*Hausa, Niger/Nigeria*)

= "Better thank God than thank the cook."

12. He passed by the milking of his mother-in-law's cattle. (*Ndebele, Zimbabwe*)

= "Not to show respect [by doing work], at least to one's mother-in-law, is very bad behaviour. Said of one who has complete disregard for the feelings of others."

13. The son-in-law who showed too much respect one day ran away with the fish. (*Sena, Malawi/Mozambique*)

= Do not trust those who always flatter.

VIII

WIDOW

1. The baobab has fallen. Now the goats start climbing on it. (*Minyanka, Mali*)

   = "A woman was respected, but her husband has just died and this makes her lose respect in the community."

2. The widow in a hurry passes by the handsome man. (*Bassar, Togo*)

3. One does not despise one's mother as a widow. (*Kundu, Cameroon*)

4. One can tell a widow only this: have patience. (*Igbo, Nigeria*)

   = "A woman is more respected when her husband is alive. No attention is paid to a woman after her husband is dead. The proverb expresses a situation of misfortune and distress."

5. A widow never fails to praise her dead husband. (*Ganda, Uganda*)

   = "In the presence of her new husband she'll say: 'He gave me so many things, clothes and so on.'"

6. Looking here and looking there, a widow ignores her husband. (*Mamprusi, Burkina Faso*)

   = "Accepting temptation leads to infidelity."

7. Even a clever woman can settle nothing the day her husband dies. (*Minyanka, Mali*)

8. You flirted with the widow, but do you know what killed her husband? (*Bassar, Togo*)

= "Warning not to marry too easily a widow."

9. One tells a widow by her hair. (*Minyanka, Mali*)

= "The widow is not allowed to dress her hair. She wears a white headband. More generally: A foreigner sees a young man on a new moped. He asks: 'Who is this? It is the eldest son of the richest family in the village, is the reply, and then the proverb is quoted. In other words: he/she is easy to recognize."

10. Preferred wives never mourn their husbands. (*Kundu, Cameroon*)

= "The preferred wife has no material problems when her husband dies, while the other wives have nothing: the world's wages are ingratitude."

11. (a) A widow does not eat fat meat. (*Kundu, Cameroon*)
(b) A widow has to calculate. (*Kundu, Cameroon*)

= "Most widows are in need, because nobody takes care of them."

12. A widow is not free for any. (*Kundu, Cameroon*)

= "According to the tradition, the widow stays in the family of the deceased husband."

13. A well-to-do widow never wants for tobacco. (*Kundu, Cameroon*)

= "The widow of a rich man who has been highly thought of does not lack anything."

14. Whether the widow has her period or not, it makes no difference. (*Baule, Ivory Coast*)

= A widow has no right to have sexual intercourse. Neither does the woman who has her period.
> High day or ordinary day, the poor man's life is always the same.

IX

GRANDMOTHER

1. Everyone knows the old woman's name, yet everyone calls her great-grandmother. (*Mamprusi, Burkina Faso*)

   = "Familiarity does not exclude respect."

2. Lacking-his-mother has sucked his grandmother. (*Fulani, Cameroon/Chad/Nigeria*)

   = "Quoted in situations where someone is forced to do what he would never have done in normal circumstances."

3. Your grandmother has taught you this and you want to ask your mother? (*Baule, Ivory Coast*)

   = "The grandmother knows better: she has formed the mother."

4. The baby nursed by the grandmother can never be corrected. (*Gikuyu, Kenya*)

   = She spoils her grandchildren.

5. One person's grandmother marries, but another one's is eaten by a crocodile. (*Fulani, Senegal*)

   = They are not alike: "Is said among women friends of the same age group as a familiar way to turn down an invitation: one needs no other excuse if the saying is quoted."

6. One man's wife is another man's grandmother. (*Fulani, Niger/ Nigeria*)

   = Not everybody is in the same position.

7. As long as her dance is not finished, don't say: "grandmother, your foot is nimble." (*Mandinka, Senegal*)

   = Don't praise the day before the evening.

X

OLD WOMAN

1. The toothless old woman still chews cola nut. (*Mamprusi, Burkina Faso*)

= "The disabled finds a way of overcoming his limitations."

2. A woman with withered breasts drinks beer like a man. (*Ganda, Uganda*)

= After menopause, women arrogate certain rights.

3. An old woman cannot be frightened by marriage. (*Fulani, Senegal*)

= "She has already experienced what it means. Is said of those who have gone through a certain danger and are no longer upset by the idea of going through it again."

4. An old calabash is still useful. (*Minyanka, Mali*)

= "If you are old, you are still valuable."

5. (a) The old woman has a reason for running in the rice field. (*Baule, Ivory Coast*)
(b) Old women do not whistle without reason. (*Rundi, Burundi*)

= "If someone uses extraordinary means, or behaves contrary to the tradition, there must be special reasons to do so. It is forbidden for women to whistle, because it brings bad luck. It is believed that old women can chase red ants by whistling."

6. An old goat never sneezes for nothing. (*Gikuyu, Kenya*)

   = "Old ones do not speak without reason, they speak the truth."

7. The head of an old woman is not shown for nothing. (*Minyanka, Mali*)

   = "Old women normally wear a kerchief and do not show their head without it. Quoted when a request is answered with another request: e.g. 'Buy me a drink first and I'll bother afterwards'."

8. The old woman who boils water for porridge does not lack grandchildren. (*Rwanda, Rwanda*)

   = "The one who has fortune, does not lack friends."

9. The old woman's goat is skinned in her sight. (*Mamprusi, Burkina Faso*)

   = "The poor are careful not to waste the little gain they have."

10. If an old woman gives a lift to another, the one on the ground is bluffing. (*Mamprusi, Burkina Faso*)

    = "Being weak but able is better than being helped and disabled."

11. Old women's footsteps start firmly but don't last. (*Rundi, Burundi*)

    = "Is said of those who lack perseverance, who are full of enthusiasm in the beginning, but whose activities soon fizzle out."

12. The old woman who must grind and cook cannot join in the evening chat. (*Minyanka, Mali*)

    = "In general women share the work, and the one who grinds is not the one who cooks. When a woman is old, she will be over head and ears in work if she is in charge of the two.
    > One cannot take care seriously of two things at the same time."

13. Worries will kill the old woman next to her basket full of fish. (*Minyanka, Mali*)

    = One dies of hunger or one dies of disgust.

14. If you see an old woman in trouble, then there's nobody taking care of her. (*Minyanka, Mali*)

= "It is unthinkable for an old woman to live alone. there is always somebody who tills the ground for her and nourishes her.
> Some youngsters want to learn French but nobody in the village knows that language. They come to Karangosso and introduce their problem to the secretary of this village by quoting the proverb."

15. An old woman falls a second time, the things in her basket will be counted. (*Igbo, Nigeria*)

= "Everybody looks forward to what he/she will do next time.
> Two failures and people will hold you responsible or begin to suspect your ability."

16. The old woman's basket does not fill itself if she's always sitting down. (*Minyanka, Mali*)

= "One has to act in daily life."

17. Old age is like being lame. (*Gikuyu, Kenya*)

= "The proverb is told by or to old women."

18. A fallen palm tree is trod upon; as long as it stands, it can choose its climbers. (*Vili, Cabinda*)

= "This pot-lid proverb expresses (in images) a wife's disappointment towards her husband: 'Long ago I was beautiful and gave myself to you alone, although I could get as many lovers as I wanted. Now I am old and ugly [fallen palm tree] and despised [foot set upon tree], but is that a reason for you to quarrel with me all the time?' "

19. When an old woman sees Death pass by and asks him to come back and pass the night, he will return and take all her children. (*Rwanda, Rwanda*)

20. Even a clever old woman will be caught by the rain when she goes out to make water. (*Minyanka, Mali*)

= "Normally a woman goes outside the village to urinate.
>Even if you are intelligent, there are things you can't do."

21. No wife will have her white hair shaved at her mother's. (*Gikuyu, Kenya*)

= "Gikuyu girls go around with bald heads which they get periodically shaved by their relations. So the woman, who by being married has left her house and relations, will never be shaved at her mother's [when she is old]."

22. The young man's eye disdains the old woman. (*Rundi, Burundi*)

= "Those who are alike, get together."

23. If you are ashamed of an old wife, you'll sleep alone. (*Baule, Ivory Coast*)

= "Do as you like and do not take to heart what other people may think."

24. When the young wife dies one returns to the old. (*Gikuyu, Kenya*)

= One acts according to one's possibilities.

25. The old woman who outstrips another one says: "Spare me those hollow eyes." (*Rwanda, Rwanda*)

= "One prides oneself on being better than others in the same situation."
>In the land of the blind the one-eyed is king.

26. If an old woman would dance, she would dress first. (*Fulani, Senegal*)

= "It is quite exceptional for an old woman to dance at all. If she wants to, she must appear in the circle neatly dressed, her hair nicely done.
>Before any enterprise one must take all necessary precautions and preparations, so as not to miss a chance."

27. If an old woman chases a rabbit, she has already killed more than one. (*Mamprusi, Burkina Faso*)

= "If a weak person is ambitious, don't think he cannot succeed."

28. The water-carrier passes by the bad old woman's door. (*Minyanka, Mali*)

= "If an old woman cannot get along with anybody, she must shift for herself."

29. Among old women there are more bad than good. (*Fulani, Senegal*)

= "Old women, if they are good, can have a good influence; bad ones disturb the home. Old women are accused of being evil tongues, bad advisers of young women and of serving as procuresses."

PART TWO

ELEMENTS OF LIFE

I

BEAUTY

1. No woman as beautiful as the docile one. (*Rwanda, Rwanda*)

2. (a) A beautiful woman cannot be scared away like the birds that eat the harvest. (*Swahili, East Africa*)
   (b) A bird can be guarded, a wife cannot. (*Swahili, East Africa*)

3. Beautiful women are like fresh banana leaves: they never come to an end in the bananary. (*Ganda, Uganda*)

   = "There will always be plenty of beautiful girls."

4. If Miss-this-year is pretty, Miss-next-year is prettier. (*Hausa, Niger/Nigeria*)

5. The running woman holds her breasts for beauty's sake, not because she thinks she'll lose them. (*Twi, Ghana*)

   = "Appearance may make you think that a person is in difficulty. It may not be the case. There may be a perfectly normal explanation. Appearances may be deceptive."

6. A woman is like the merino sheep: her beauty is judged by her backside. (*Sotho, South Africa/Lesotho*)

7. (a) The handsome finger gets the ring. (*Swahili, East Africa*)
   (b) Born beautiful, born married. (*Idem*)

   = "The person who deserves esteem will get it."

8. When a woman takes a long time bathing, be sure she is decking herself out. (*Ashanti, Ghana*)

55

9. Beauty does not reside in the butter pot. (*Rundi, Burundi*)

    = "Artifices do not produce beauty."

10. Beauty is half a God-given favour; intelligence a whole one. (*Fulani, Senegal/Gambia*)

11. A woman's beauty is not in her face. (*Swahili, Tanzania*)

12. With or without a nose-plug, women are always beautiful. (*Makua, Mozambique*)

13. There is nothing that is not the breast of a woman. (*Zulu, South Africa/Swaziland*)

    = "Every woman, whatever her appearance, will have someone who will admire her."

14. Woman's beauty is a cloud's beauty. (*Fang/Bulu, Cameroon/Gabon*)

15. Beauty is an empty calabash. (*Kundu, Cameroon*)

    = "The outside may be beautiful, but inside there may be nothing."

16. The young woman is beautiful, but her heart is an *inkengi* rat. (*Mongo, Zaïre*)

    = "Beauty can be dangerous."

17. You do not suffer hunger, though a beautiful woman leaves you. (*Ganda, Uganda*)

    = "You can get another to cook for you."

18. The beautiful woman will bring diseases. (*Bassar, Togo*)

    = Used to warn young ones.

19. (a) Marry a beauty, marry trouble. (*Kru, Liberia; Mande, Sierra Leone*)
    (b) A beautiful woman leaves trouble behind. (*Ganda, Uganda*)
    (c) A beautiful woman is the sister of many. (*Ganda, Uganda*)

    = "Everybody likes to claim relationship with her."

20. A beautiful woman is like a well-polished drum: it kills those who fight hardest for it. (*Ganda, Uganda*)

= "They all try to get it by fighting and may die for it. Applied to a number of wooers [suitors], all trying to win the same beautiful lady."

21. The wife with beautiful hair is like a leopard. (*Mongo, Zaïre*)

= "Beautiful but dangerous."

22. Our neighbour's daughter looks beautiful to those across the river. (*Tonga, Zambia*)

= "Certain things look much more beautiful and charming from afar than they really are."

23. A very beautiful woman is either a witch or a prostitute. (*Sara, Chad*)

24. If a girl says No to marriage, just wait for her breasts to sag. (*Rundi, Burundi*)

= Then she'll no longer cause you trouble.
> Laughs best who laughs last.

I I

LOVE

1. He that a woman avoids, she loves. (*Yoruba, Nigeria*)

2. A woman is a *ntsatsi*; you never know where it falls. (*Sena, Malawi*)

   = "One can never predetermine with whom a woman will fall in love. She is like the pod of the *ntsatsi* tree: impossible to predetermine where its seed will fall when the pod explodes."

3. She-in-love has abandoned her child and carries her husband on her back. (*Rwanda, Rwanda*)

   = "Passion blinds."

4. If a woman does not love you, she calls you brother. (*Baule, Ivory Coast*)

   = "So she cannot sleep with you."

5. Not even God is ripe enough to catch a woman in love. (*Yoruba, Nigeria*)

   = Women in love outmanœuvre anyone.

6. Woman is three things: she you love, she who loves you and she you want to possess. (*Wolof, Senegal*)

7. (a) Naïve and silly, the bride calls marriage "love". (*Ganda, Uganda*)
   (b) Wedlock is not "love me". (*Kundu, Cameroon*)

   = "Many see their mistake soon."

8. Love for a girl lies below the navel. (*Rwanda, Rwanda*)

= "One likes things for their utility. The utility of a woman is to bear children."

9. Who loves the mother must love the child. (*Bemba, Zambia*)

= "If you love a woman, love also her children, though they may not be yours. This applies especially to somebody who marries a 'second-hand' wife."

10. A wife you love for her being, not for her beauty. (*Swahili, Kenya*)

11. If the king's wife does not fall in love with you, you elude much trouble. (*Dendi, Benin*)

= "Divine protection."

12. Illicit love spoils the uncircumcised girl. (*Gikuyu, Kenya*)

= "Sexual relations between an uncircumcised girl and a circumcised young man are considered unmentionable depravity by the Gikuyu."

13. If you love a woman, you cultivate for the soothsayer. (*Rwanda, Rwanda*)

= "Blind love makes you poor." One may consult different soothsayers and thus spend a lot of money.

14. A happy girl thinks that hers must be better. (*Rwanda, Rwanda*)

= "Hers" means her vagina. "The lucky one attributes his good luck to his own merits."

15. The woman too eager to make the bed will not notice that she does not please. (*Rwanda, Rwanda*)

= "Passion makes blind."

16. Killing himself for one woman, he misses thousands of others. (*Yoruba, Nigeria*)

17. (a) You want to have no wife, then get one quickly; don't get one quickly, you'll get a wife. (*Yoruba, Nigeria*)
(b) Quick to love, quick not to love. (*Yoruba, Nigeria*)

18. You ask a girl in marriage, you marry a love-potion. (*Rwanda, Rwanda*)

= "Infusions and amulets are used to appeal or keep a person of the other sex by magic means."

19. If you really love your wife, you have to beat her. (*Tigrinya, Ethiopia*)

III

SEX

1. A new sleeping-mat is no pleasure to sleep on. (*Swahili, East Africa*)

   = "A young wife has a lot to learn."

2. If you want to make love, first look for a mat. (*Baule, Ivory Coast*)

   = "If you want to realize your plans, first find the right means."

3. You gave me a wife without giving me a mat. (*Bassar, Togo*)

   = "Said when one receives something incomplete."

4. If you carve a harp-lute, you must know how to play it. (*Ngbaka, Central African Republic*)

   = "If you marry a woman, you must know how to use her."

5. If you feel her thigh, don't fear her sex. (*Mandinka, Gambia/ Senegal*)

   = "When you take an initiative, don't hesitate to continue."

6. Getting used to potato leaves made one dig for the potatoes. (*Chewa, Malawi*)

   = "One must not get accustomed to something – even if it is not wrong – if it can lead to something bad. For instance, friendship between a boy and a girl – which is not bad – might lead to intimacies which might bring undesired pregnancies."

7. A woman is like the legs of a hide: if you don't rub them, they won't become soft. (*Ganda, Uganda*)

8. Sitting on her heel, the woman closes the entrance to numerous offspring. (*Rwanda, Rwanda*)

= Literally: she bars the access to her uterus that way.
> "Frigidity is a handicap to the prosperity of the lineage."

9. If the girl has appointed a day to her fiancé, that day she must open up her hips. (*Minyanka, Mali*)

= "One has to keep his promises, even if it is difficult."

10. An eager girl makes love though she has been asked in marriage. (*Rwanda, Rwanda*)

11. "Let-me-please! Let-me-please!" will graze the vagina. (*Rwanda, Rwanda*)

= "If you want to please everybody, you harm yourself."

12. The kind woman has a hairless vagina. (*Mamprusi, Burkina Faso*)

= "For a woman to have abundant hair on her private parts is a sign of health and fertility.
> Kind people are not wealthy."

13. Who gets one for nothing calls it nothing. (*Rwanda, Rwanda*)

= "One" here means vagina: "something you get without effort has no value."

14. (a) If a woman offers her sex to everyone, pestles are used on it. (*Minyanka, Mali*)
(b) Because of her goodness, a woman's sex was carried off by a dog. (*Bete, Ivory Coast*)

= If you are too confident or naïve, you'll always be abused by swindlers and/or despised.

15. The wild beast cannot live with the lamb. (*Bari, Sudan*)

= "A girl who runs into somebody's house cannot stay untouched."

16. No girl ever died without being told: "Turn my way." (*Rwanda, Rwanda*)

= "No girl is so ugly that she cannot find a husband. 'Turning my way' is a euphemism for making love."

17. As long as he owns a woman, he doesn't lie with his back turned. (*Mamprusi, Burkina Faso*)

= "A man wouldn't refuse what is his own to enjoy."

18. The bell needs its tongue. (*Gikuyu, Kenya*)

= "The woman needs a man."

19. Even if your wife's sex is small, dawn will find you there. (*Minyanka, Mali*)

= "One uses and appreciates the few things one owns."

20. Better a short penis than sleeping alone. (*Baule, Ivory Coast*)

21. (a) Not all little seats are good to occupy. (*Mandinka, The Gambia/Senegal*)
(b) Not all nice houses are good to spend the night in. (*Bambara, Mali*)

= Advice given to young men: "One should not make love to all beautiful women: some may have diseases."

22. Never sleep with a woman who lightens her skin. (*Lingala, Zaïre*)

= Do not trust such a woman.

23. The mouth seeks a wife for the penis. (*Mamprusi, Burkina Faso*)

= "Flattery is needed to get something from another for one's own enjoyment."

24. Do not despise a woman you have not undressed. (*Bemba, Zambia*)

= "Never condemn or judge somebody before you know what he is doing or talking about, just as you would never call a woman useless or impotent before you have undressed her and slept with her."

25. A woman hides the penis, but she won't hide the belly. (*Mamprusi, Burkina Faso*)

= "The origins may be secret but the outcome will be public."

26. The woman who has spent the night with her husband shows it in the way they greet. (*Minyanka, Mali*)

   = "In the polygamous system, wives go in turn to their husband's room. The morning greetings between wife and husband are different for the one whose turn it has been.
   > Quoted, for instance, when a man arrives looking happy. One greets him and says the proverb, meaning: 'You certainly bring good news.' "

27. The husband of a lazy wife: his nights are good, his day bad. (*Minyanka, Mali*)

   = "During the day time a wife must cook and bring food to her husband in the field. The proverb stigmatizes laziness."

28. The mother of twins does not fear a huge penis. (*Baule, Ivory Coast*)

29. If you drink the neighbour's wine, don't take away his calabash. (*Ngbaka, Central African Republic*)

   = "A man who makes love to someone else's wife must not force her to leave her husband."

30. A woman who roves never fails to get a child. (*Gikuyu, Kenya*)

   = "So, girls, stay at home and behave.
   > The proverb refers to married women who, failing to have children of their husbands, go around looking for other men."

31. If you want sex while travelling, travel with your wife. (*Minyanka, Mali*)

   = "This is the best way to prevent all kinds of problems.
   > One is always best served by oneself."

32. Woman is like a corn cob: you have no teeth, you hardly eat. (*Fang, Gabon/Cameroon*)

33. The impotent man does not eat seasoned food. (*Lunda, Angola/Zambia/Zaïre*)

   = "When a person does not do his duties, he is not entitled to any remuneration. It is like the impotent man who either cannot find a wife to cook for him, or has one but she refuses to cook for him because he fails to fulfil his marital duties."

34. When the sex falls ill, it is its owner's alone. (*Yoruba, Benin*)

   = "Use without abuse."

I V

PREGNANCY/CHILDBIRTH

1. It takes a man to break the bed; a woman alone cannot. (*Lunda, Angola/Zambia/Zaïre*)

   = "A woman can only become pregnant by sleeping with a man. A pregnancy before marriage is less respected than after marriage."

2. A fire and a pregnancy cannot be kept secret. (*Rwanda, Rwanda*)

   = "It is stupid to try to hide what manifests itself naturally."

3. Better a bad dowry than a bad gift. (*Fulani, Senegal*)

   = "Misalliance is better than illegitimate pregnancy."

4. A girl gets pregnant only once. (*Rwanda, Rwanda*)

   = "As soon as her child is born she has become woman. Quoted by somebody to emphasize that he'll not commit some foolishness again."

5. Wombs see trouble. (*Ganda, Uganda*)

   = "Parents often experience trouble with their children."

6. A woman who brings forth takes trouble upon herself. (*Ganda, Uganda*)

7. Give birth to children, you'll be pregnant with worries. (*Ovambo/Oshiwambo, Namibia*)

8. No man can fool a pregnant woman. (*Fulani, Senegal*)

   = "Having gone through a certain experience, one has learnt something."

65

9. Two pregnant women cannot carry each other. (*Mandinka, Mali*)

= "Two people infatuated by their own qualities do not stop talking about their personal merits and do not listen to each other, so the conversation ends in a row. In such a situation somebody quotes the proverb."

10. A pregnant woman is not sent away. (*Mongo, Zaïre*)

= Her child will strengthen the community.

11. A wife is in the man's compound for the sake of the child. (*Mamprusi, Burkina Faso*)

= She is there to give her husband children.
> "Efforts are made for the sake of prospective gain."

12. The pregnant woman does not see her lower belly. (*Baule, Ivory Coast*)

= Each act has its consequences.

13. Do not fasten the baby strap while the child is in his mother's belly. (*Ngbaka, Central African Republic*)

= "There is a firm belief that if one manufactures the leather strap in which the mother carries the baby on her hip, before the child is born, he/she will not be born alive or not live. The proverb is used in a much more general sense: One should not count one's chickens before they are hatched."

14. (a) Do not call the pregnant woman a mother. (*Baule, Ivory Coast*)
(b) Pregnancy doesn't yet mean baby. (*Baule, Ivory Coast*)

15. A pregnant wife shouldn't scorn a co-wife's child. (*Mamprusi, Burkina Faso*)

= "Don't underrate someone's achievement if you are about to try the same thing."

16. (a) A mother should not scoff at a woman in labour. (*Rundi, Burundi*)
(b) Only an ignorant girl laughs at a littering sheep. (*Rundi, Burundi*)

= "Don't laugh at other people's misfortunes."

17. Birth pains near the mortar, one of the women will soon give birth. (*Fulani, Senegal*)

= "Also. if you see a man enter a flock. it is a butcher in search of a good animal to slaughter. According to the situation. the use. the profession. one knows what a person is going to do. This is often very useful and it should be that way in a well-regulated society where traditions and customs are respected."

18. A woman in childbirth trembles, if somebody is there to help her. (*Ganda, Uganda*)

    = "If nobody is there, she does not tremble and helps herself." Is quoted when somebody is exaggerating his trouble, sickness, etc.

19. Insult the midwife, and who will help you next time? (*Sena, Malawi/Mozambique*)

    = "If you show ingratitude to people who help you, you are digging your own grave. Nobody will help you next time."

20. If you are impatient to have a child, you marry a pregnant woman. (*Fulani, Senegal*)

    = "Is said of those who in their thirst for money do not shrink from any means, be it theft of swindling."

21. One does not force a pregnant woman to give birth. (*Baule, Ivory Coast*)

    = No remedy but patience.

22. The woman who gives birth is like the banana tree: it breaks under the weight of its fruit. (*Gikuyu, Kenya*)

    = "Maternity means pain to the mother."

23. Her husband away, a woman can bear, but she cannot conceive. (*Baule, Ivory Coast*)

    = "To judge a man, he has to be present."

24. A woman who has borne children is like a used potato plot: from time to time one can dig up some potatoes. (*Ganda, Uganda*)

25. A foolish mother thinks her only child her seventh. (*Rwanda, Rwanda*)

= "The seventh child and the next ones were considered as beings who attract misfortune. Their birth must be surrounded by special purification rites. Thus. at the birth of their seventh child the parents were risking blindness and conjured the danger by wearing special amulets.
> The behaviour of the fool is extravagant."

26. Who gives birth gets many gifts. (*Rundi, Burundi*)

= "Everybody congratulates one who succeeds in an enterprise or overcomes a problem."

27. One who has given birth does not wither. (*Kundu, Cameroon*)

28. A mother of twins must have a belly. (*Kundu, Cameroon*)

29. Childbirth will later lighten your burden. (*Ovambo/Oshiwambo, Namibia*)

30. The womb is like the *muwogo* plant: it brings forth both beautiful and ugly. (*Ganda, Uganda*)

= "On the same *muwogo* or cassava plant one finds good and bad tubers. Intended as a consolation for the mother."

31. One womb can give birth to a thief and a poisoner. (*Gikuyu, Kenya*)

= "Parents should not be blamed for the evils of their bad children."

32. A woman who bears an ugly child, must offer to the *lubaale*. (*Ganda, Uganda*)

= The *lubaale* is the oracle. The offering is meant "to secure the protection of the lubaale."

33. A woman whose belly is covered in pimples never gives birth to a child with hairy legs. (*Mandinka, Guinea*)

= "A bad woman can hardly beget a valuable child."

34. They despise the unsightly woman, and she brings forth a splendid little boy. (*Ganda, Uganda*)

= "They never expected she still could produce a son and heir."

35. A child is the girdle of marriage. (*Tumbuka, Malawi*)

= "If a family has no children. the partners run the risk of breaking up. but when parents see their reflection in their children they feel more the sense of oneness: marriage is just tied more firmly."

36. A woman who cannot keep a live child blames God. (*Afar, Ethiopia*)

= The loser always finds a scapegoat.

37. Many births, many burials. (*Gikuyu, Kenya*)

= "In the family where there are many children one must expect many griefs too.
> People who run many businesses must expect many reverses."

V

STERILITY

1. Breasts are like a beard: even the barren woman has them. (*Ganda, Uganda*)

   = "A beard can be worn by one who has got a family, and by one who has not." Breasts are no guarantee.
   > Appearances can be deceptive.

2. Who cannot tell her barrenness will pay her dowry. (*Rwanda, Rwanda*)

   "One should verify the effectiveness of the means if one wants to secure one's object."

3. The chance of motherhood fades with regular menstruation. (*Mboshi, Congo*)

   = "Chances of success diminish as time goes by."

4. Beauty without children cannot prosper. (*Mongo, Zaïre*)

   = "If your wife is beautiful but you have no children, you will not be successful in life. It's children that enrich you."

5. The childless one anoints herself before she goes out to chop firewood. (*Rwanda, Rwanda*)

   = "The woman who has got no children embellishes herself, but she cannot stay elegant for long because of the numerous tasks she has to fulfil all alone: no children to help her."

6. A barren woman is like a hornless goat: when it slips its halter, you no longer have a hold on it. (*Ganda, Uganda*)

   = "If she leaves her husband, she won't come back to him."

7. The one whose children are buried in her womb will not see their graves. (*Rundi, Burundi*)

   = "The sterile woman does not even have the comfort of weeping on the graves of her children."

8. The child of a *mugumba* does not die a natural death. (*Ganda, Uganda*)

   "Not only a woman who has no children is called a *mugumba*, but also one whose childen die soon after birth. She is constantly afraid that her child is being bewitched."

9. The woman whose sons have died is richer than a barren woman. (*Gikuyu, Kenya*)

10. The barren woman gets visitors. (*Ganda, Uganda*)

    = She is exploited because she is defenceless.

11. A useless person is like a woman both lazy and barren. (*Ganda, Uganda*)

    = "She does not work and cannot produce any children."

12. Miscarriage is not sterility. (*Minyanka, Mali*)

    = "Next time will be better."

13. A barren woman should not scorn a bad child. (*Minyanka, Burkina Faso*)

    = "If you can't do it, don't insult someone who hasn't done it well."

14. Where the mother sends the children, there goes the childless one herself. (*Ganda, Uganda*)

15. Who will draw water for the childless old woman? (*Gikuyu, Kenya*)

16. Who has no work to do can dig the spinster's grave. (*Minyanka, Mali*)

    = "The woman who never married and the one who returned home after a brief marriage are despised. Sterile, they are buried without dignity. No husband takes care of her and nobody is interested in protecting or burying them. Quoted by someone who does not want to be disturbed in a serious work: he has other things to do."

VI

WORK

1. Regular work tires a woman but totally wrecks a man. (*Fang, Cameroon/Gabon/Equatorial Guinea*)

2. To the active woman man will belong. (*Fulani, Senegal*)

   = "The good housewife does with her husband as she likes."

3. A mother's back sins when it is seated. (*Rundi, Burundi*)

   = A mother is wrong when she neglects her children; she is not to be blamed when she loses them in spite of her good care and hard work.

4. Women take up their market baskets and bundles of gossip. (*Efik, Nigeria; Kongo, Zaïre*)

5. The mother may be ugly, but she goes into the bush to work. (*Kongo, Zaïre*)

   = "Mothers are good for work."

6. Does a man set up a plantation without a wife? (*Ganda, Uganda*)

7. A woman diligent in the garden will see the chickens dancing. (*Ganda, Uganda*)

   = "Plenty of insects from the freshly cultivated grounds, remnants of eatable roots are ever there."

8. The lazy one is pregnant in the sowing season. (*Rundi, Burundi*)

9. A diligent woman brings forth food; a lazy one brings weeds. (*Ganda, Uganda*)

10. She whose seedlings have not germinated doesn't throw down the seed container. (*Gikuyu, Kenya*)

= "You just do not give up even if you have not had instant success."

11. The woman's trills are shouted at the mortar. (*Gikuyu, Kenya*)

= "Refers to the songs and shouts of the women crushing the sugar cane to be brewed; and means that such songs are sung only at that occasion."

12. A woman sells garden-eggs, not gunpowder. (*Ashanti, Ghana*)

= Women should do work that is appropriate to them and not interfere in men's affairs.

13. (a) A bad home sends you for water and fire wood. (*Rwanda, Rwanda*)
(b) Beaten up by his wife, Shyirambere says: "Give me a pitcher, I will go and draw water." (*Idem*)

= "The husband dominated by his wife becomes her slave. Drawing water is women's or children's work."

14. Don't interrupt a woman fetching water. (*Namibia*)

= "Water is vital for the household."
> Do not disturb someone who has to accomplish a delicate task.

15. Produce your wrinkles and who will eat your beans? (*Yaka, Zaïre*)

= "Women must serve in a good humour."

16. Don't blame the cooks. (*Ganda, Uganda*)

= "So one says, if he has had nothing to eat, where he came from. He hopes to get food here. Therefore he tries to curry favour with the cooks."

17. What explodes in the pot won't kill a man. (*Rwanda, Rwanda*)

= "Cooking matters are women's concern. Men should not worry about them.
> Everybody has his duties."

18. The food of a woman who speaks sweetly will never be rejected by her husband. (*Igbo, Nigeria*)

= "One good turn deserves another. Politeness is often rewarded with politeness."

19. The stew which the husband does not like should not be prepared by the wife. (*Yoruba, Nigeria*)

20. A woman who wants something for her stew will not give up looking until she finds it. (*Yoruba, Nigeria*)

= "Recommends industry and perseverance: Just as the woman will not be satisfied until her stew has all the proper ingredients, so should a person not be satisfied with whatever he does until he does it as it should be done."

21. The useless woman puts on a millstone without using it. (*Gen, Benin*)

22. The greedy-guts discourages the woman who grinds. (*Rundi, Burundi*)

23. Better go to sleep hungry than wait for food prepared by a woman having her period. (*Baule, Ivory Coast*)

= "During her periods a woman does not prepare food for other people."

24. She who offers a half-cooked meal is better than she who offers her buttocks. (*Rwanda, Rwanda*)

= "A hard-working but awkward wife is better than a lazy one."

25. Even a good woman cook is a failure once. (*Minyanka, Mali*)

= "Everybody makes a mistake or breaks a tool while at work."

26. It is not because women draw water from the same well that their sauces taste the same. (*Baule, Ivory Coast*)

27. A hard-working wife will make you eat with a shield over your food. (*Ganda, Uganda*)

= "When you have eaten enough and she wants to dish up more food, you hold the hand in the form of a shield over the food. You are really satisfied."

28. He who asks for mashed food has someone to mash it. (*Gikuyu, Kemya*)

= "Unless a man has a wife, he cannot expect well-cooked food."

29. The prostitute's breadwinner is her bottom. (*Minyanka, Mali*)

= "Her profession makes her behave the way she does."

30. Who has harvested in time of famine will always find a wife. (*Rundi, Burundi*)

= He certainly is a genius.

31. The married chicken pecks, the unmarried chicken pecks. Better not to be married then: she'll peck for herself. (*Fulani, Senegal*)

32. The wife is a wife because of hands. (*Zulu, South Africa/ Swaziland*)

= A wife should be handy, skilful in practical work.

33. When the male soul is alive, the female soul does not crack nuts. (*Ashanti, Ghana*)

34. When a woman makes the giant drum, it is kept in the man's room. (*Idem*)

= "Society has not assigned those roles to women. If they insist on performing male roles, the glory will go to the man and the women will not get any appreciation for their extra efforts."

35. The faggot brought home by the woman becomes the cat-o'nine-tails that beats her. (*Sara, Chad*)

VII

QUARRELS

1. He who is not smart in speech and argument should not take a talkative wife. (*Yoruba, Nigeria*)

2. To marry a woman is to marry palavers. (*Kongo, Zaïre*)

3. Quarrelling is peculiar to the woman with sons. (*Gikuyu, Kenya*)

   = "Mothers are more proud of their sons than of their daughters and thus are inclined to quarrel in order to defend or exalt their sons."

4. A woman with debts is a quarrelsome woman. (*Gikuyu, Kenya*)

   = Her debts make her quarrelsome.

5. (a) Women's quarrels never end. (*Gikuyu, Kenya*)

   = "Avoid quarrels with women."

   (b) Men's anger does not last like women's. (*Gikuyu, Kenya*)

   = "Women are as prone to revenge injuries as men to forgive them."

   (c) Women sow discord. (*Luba, Zaïre*)

6. If a woman enters the market place and keeps quiet, it goes well; she utters one word, people start beating each other. (*Mossi, Burkina Faso*)

7. Better to sleep in the heat of the sun than to be with a quarrelsome wife. (*Karaboro, Ivory Coast*)

8. (a) Where the wife speaks, the knife will resound. (*Rwanda, Rwanda*)

76

= "The home where the wife behaves like a man perishes."

(b) **The wife who does not listen to her husband may cause his death.** (*Banen, Cameroon*)

= "Refers to a story where a bad wife made her husband leave the hut to escape her palavers; in the night he was then killed by enemies."

9. **A lazy and touchy woman does not feed her husband well.** (*Ganda, Uganda*)

10. **The woman who does not prepare food is satiated by slandering and dies by co-wives' gossiping.** (*Mongo, Zaïre*)

11. (a) **The beans of the jealous woman overcook in the pot.** (*Mamprusi, Burkina Faso*)

= "Jealousy brings you to neglect your duty."

(b) **A woman without sense indulges in jealousy.** (*Mamprusi, Burkina Faso*)

= "Not wise to be jealous."

12. **A bad woman gets sent back to her relatives.** (*Rundi, Burundi*)

13. **Jealousy is calmed down by: "Get out from here, I have repudiated you."** (*Fulani, Senegal*)

= "Is quoted to a jealous man to make him understand that the best way to regain tranquillity is to repudiate his wife."

14. **The *ngongongo* bird fishes in the lake and says: "I only fish."** (*Vili, Cabinda*)

= Pot-lid message sent by a woman as a peace proposal to the angry wife of a man she has taken up with for a while. The fishing bird sculpted on the lid means: "Let's stay friends, I did not mean to take your husband away. I only fished for a while and leave the lake to you."

15. **Woman's urine should not pass the threshold.** (*Kundu, Cameroon*)

= "Woman's quarrels should stay inside the house."

16. The pain of women is on their hips. (*Swahili, East Africa*)

= "Muttered by a vexed husband against a nagging wife. Women [thus a husband told me] will use the children as an excuse for quarrelling and complaining. Women carry their children on their hips."

17. If a wife has put her husband in the cooking-pot her children simmer. (*Fulani, Senegal*)

= "The wife who behaves badly with her husband is punished in her children, who follow her bad example and will become bad too."

18. Claim-beatings-again tells her husband he is castrated. (*Rwanda, Rwanda*)

= "Brawlers often become the victims of quarrels they provoke themselves."

19. Give your wife only half of what she demands; otherwise she'll blame you for having given her all. (*Fulani, Niger*)

20. Is he still arrogant? His wife will throw him to the ground, and he will grow a hunchback. (*Yoruba, Nigeria*)

= "It would be considered a great disgrace for a man to be thrown by his wife. The proverb contains the suggestion that the person who does not learn humility will one day be disgraced and thus forced to learn humility the hard way."

21. Women's strife will cost no sheep. (*Gikuyu, Kenya*)

= "According to Gikuyu custom, the one who wounds another in a quarrel must pay a sheep as a fine. The proverb means that in women's strifes nobody incurs such a fine, for their quarrels are usually words only. Words are for women, actions for men."

22. Two buttocks cannot avoid brushing. (*Tonga, Zambia*)

= "People living together cannot avoid occasional elbow-brushing, misunderstandings and quarrels."

VIII

UNFAITHFULNESS/ UNRELIABILITY

1. A woman is nobody's relative. (*Mongo, Zaïre*)

= She marries into the family of her husband.

2. Woman is a path: don't ask who has walked on it or who will walk on it. (*Wolof, Senegal*)

3. (a) If you marry the woman you meet on the dance-floor, she'll someday go off with a drummer. (*Yoruba, Nigeria*)

= "A woman of loose morals will always remain a woman of loose morals. The type of woman mentioned follows a travelling band of musicians around and dances wherever they play. A man would be foolish to marry such a woman, for she will not be faithful to him."

(b) Do not buy a woman on dancing day. (*Kundu, Cameroon*)
(c) If a woman is left to herself, a dancer will marry her. (*Fulani, Senegal*)

4. A woman is like a rat: even if it grows up in your home, it steals from you. (*Ganda, Uganda*)

= "She is not to be trusted: even after being married a long time, she might run away with somebody else."

5. (a) An unworthy woman betrays you while offering her arm as a pillow. (*Rwanda, Rwanda*)
(b) Better a mortal enemy than an unworthy woman. (*Rwanda, Rwanda*)

6. Woman is fresh water that kills, shallow water that drowns. (*Fulani, Senegal*)

= "Women are perfidious and dangerous beings with deceitful looks."

7. (a) Who follows a woman's plan will drown himself. (*Fulani, Senegal*)
    (b) Women's advice ends up in: "Oh, that I had known!" (*Hausa, Niger/Nigeria*)
    (c) He who listened to women suffered from famine at harvest time. (*Tonga, Zambia*)

    = "One must not put too much weight in the words of a woman. Doing so may lead him into trouble later on."

    (d) Should I believe a woman? Better ally oneself with death. (*Fon, Benin*)

8. Believe a woman's word the day after. (*Gikuyu, Kenya*)

    = "Don't trust a woman's word until you've reviewed it overnight."

9. A woman can't help telling lies. (*Ganda, Uganda*)

10. Women have only crooked words. (*Gikuyu, Kenya*)

    = "Women keep no secrets and seldom tell the truth."

11. A woman will tell ninety-nine lies, but the hundredth will betray her. (*Hausa, Niger/Nigeria*)

12. (a) The banana tree is felled by the wind; friendship is felled by a married woman. (*Ntomba, Zaïre*)
    (b) If friendship includes the wife, it will perish. (*Kundu, Cameroon*)

13. Another man's wife is like the mongoose skin: only one person can sit on it. (*Luba, Zaïre*)

14. One does not taste another man's wife. (*Bassar, Togo*)

15. Married women are like elephant tusks: don't touch them. (*Swahili, Kenya*)

16. If you cure your enemy's penis, he'll use it to impregnate your wife. (*Mamprusi, Burkina Faso*)

    = "The very way you help someone is the way he will be wicked to you."

17. A woman does not leap over the enclosure unless she wants to divorce. (*Rundi, Burundi*)

= She destroys the home by being unfaithful.

18. The desiring vagina dies by making a bed for herself on the road. (*Rwanda, Rwanda*)

= "The debauchee turns out badly."

19. What a woman gets by prostitution, she calls gifts from her husband's relatives. (*Igbo, Nigeria*)

20. A prostitute does not recommend marriage. (*Wolof, Senegal*)

= Married women are her rivals.

21. The man who will not marry a woman with other admirers, will not marry a woman. (*Yoruba, Nigeria*)

= "In anything a person does, there is bound to be some competition. Someone who looks for a situation in which he will have no competitors will never find it: ideal situations do not exist."

22. A woman is like a cluster of palm nuts: if it falls it grows leaves. (*Baule, Ivory Coast*)

= "A woman who leaves her husband to travel will inevitably stick to some man. If women had made this proverb, it would certainly have started by the word 'man' instead."

23. Never follow an evil woman to her home. (*Rwanda, Rwanda*)

24. Woman is not a chicken cage you hang on your shoulder. (*Bassar, Togo*)

= "One can never be sure of one's wife. It is impossible to carry her everywhere and control her. Going to the fields, men take their chickens and chicks with them locked up in a cage."

25. Since olden times, little birds go and find the fields before dawn. But the fields cannot, for sure, stand up and chase the little birds. (*Fulani, Senegal*)

= "Quoted with regard to bad women. Normally it is man who courts woman, but not woman pursuing man herself."

26. (a) You can trust your brother, your father, your mother, but never your wife. (*Yoruba, Benin*)
(b) If you do not know the traitor, rely upon your wife. (*Rwanda, Rwanda*)
(c) Love your wife but do not trust her. (*Wolof, Senegal*)

27. All women are unfaithful; it's only the excessively unfaithful that people call harlot. (*Yoruba, Nigeria*)

28. If your mother cooks for you, eat: if she plans for you, refuse. (*Fulani, Senegal*)

= "A woman is only good to take care of the household and children. Never follow her advice."

29. If your wife is unfaithful, it does not mean that you sleep alone. (*Ashanti, Ghana*)

30. Who has paid the dowry for a wicked one spends the night with her. (*Rwanda, Rwanda*)

= "One has to accept the consequences of one's acts."

31. (a) One wheedles the bad woman, but draws children from her. (*Minyanka, Mali*)

= "A woman is vicious but the children are not. So she has not only disadvantages.
> Not all is bad in a given situation or in a person, man, woman."

(b) One keeps a wicked woman because of the children. (*Idem*)

= "Children and the hope for new births forbear divorce. Even the little bits of work they do profits."

32. Better fool your excisor than your hairdresser. (*Fulani, Senegal*)

= "Excision only happens once in your life, while at least once every month women need to have their hair done. Thus to fall out with one's excisor has no consequences, but it does when one is at variance with the woman who does one's hair.
> A lover is of little use, his gifts are rare, while the husband who takes care of his wives gives constantly. Thus it is better for a woman to keep her word vis-à-vis her husband than vis-à-vis her lover. The proverb is also often quoted between people when one of them failed to keep his or her word or to come to an appointment etc."

82

33. Women are the devil's snares. (*Arabic, Somalia*)

= "Turn away from them, pay no heed to them, and abandon their places of song. Achieve instead the success and strength which God gives, the Builder of the Throne."

34. Take woman for what she is: a sister of the devil. (*Yoruba, Benin*)

35. Woman is the source of all evil; only our soul saves us from the harm she does. (*Fon, Benin*)

IX

WITCHCRAFT/POISONING

1. To eat with a woman means to eat with a witch. (*Lingala and Kongo, Zaïre*)

= "Suspect the feelings of your wife."

2. A witch does not swallow bones. (*Kundu, Cameroon*)

= Witches do not kill thin, bony people. "It is only healthy, strong people that are bewitched."

3. She whose children die is a poisoner. (*Rundi, Burundi*)

= "The woman who has no children is accused of ill-nature and poisoning."

4. To marry a witch is to enter the forest with the devil. (*Baule, Ivory Coast*)

5. The professional woman shows herself by touching her own belly. (*Rwanda, Rwanda*)

= "The wicked one only feels what his wickedness means when he undergoes himself the consequences. Professional woman is a euphemism for poisoner. To touch one's own belly is a euphemism for killing one of one's own children."

6. Your wife is your favourite but also your killer. (*Mamprusi, Burkina Faso*)

= "The person with whom you are on intimate terms betrays and defeats you."

7. The professional poisoner kills her husband if she does not kill her child. (*Rundi, Burundi*)

= "Who keeps poison in her house risks one of her own family taking it accidentally."

84

8. Beware the woman who goes out at night: she is a poisonous snare, she will destroy your heart. (*Umbundu, Angola*)

= "She incarnates the devil's temptations. Because of white cloth or in her nakedness, children believe she is a spirit: they are scared. Men are seduced and fall in the snare she prepared with all ensuing disasters."

9. The witch cried yesterday; a child died today. (*Yoruba, Nigeria*)

10. You refer to witchcraft, the old woman replies: "It is raining." (*Mamprusi, Burkina Faso*)

= "The word *soo* means 'witchcraft' and 'rainy season'. It is usually old women who are accused of witchcraft. One always feigns to misunderstand when one is being accused."

11. If smallpox has killed the witch's child, let the women with children not laugh. (*Minyanka, Mali*)

= "Women always fear that a witch will harm their children. In each village some woman has the reputation of being a witch.
> Watch out for possible revenge."

12. If a beautiful woman does not steal, she catches you. (*Mamprusi, Burkina Faso*)

= "An excessively beautiful woman, like many other people who exceed the norms, is often accused of witchcraft; hence, she catches you.
> Attractive appearances always hide some wickedness."

13. Who has a co-wife will always say: "My child has been poisoned." (*Rwanda, Rwanda*)

= "One first suspects suspicious characters if one's child has been poisoned."

14. If evil is to come, it speaks through a despised woman. (*Ganda, Uganda*)

= "They will not take notice of her and will take no precautions."

15. No fetish so sacred as the woman-mother. (*Yoruba, Benin*)

= "All fetishes and all witchcraft are inferior to the woman-mother: she is the strongest."

X

POWER

1. Never marry a woman with bigger feet than your own. (*Sena, Malawi/Mozambique*)

   = Men do not like their women to be cleverer than them.

2. (a) A little string binds a big parcel. (*Ngbaka, Central African Republic*)
   (b) A small squirrel can lift up a big nut. (*Ngbaka, Central African Republic*)
   (c) The small hawk can carry off a big chick. (*Ngbaka, Central African Republic*)

   = "A small man can very well marry a big woman." These three proverbs may also refer to "a particular aspect of social organization in which a widow is remarried to a relative of her deceased husband's lineage. Often she is betrothed to a young bachelor of this lineage. When the difference in age between the new spouses is not too great, this arrangement is satisfactory for all. In case the woman is much older than the young man, he cannot refuse her. The proverb means that even a very young man can, without any problem, satisfy an older and experienced woman."
   And, more generally > "The smallest of the strong ones is more powerful than the biggest of the weak ones."

3. A woman knows her own husband but not his master. (*Afar, Ethiopia*)

   = "She doesn't think in terms of him having one: he is her master."

4. (a) The man comes out of childhood, the woman stays in womanhood. (*Gikuyu, Kenya*)

   = "According to Gikuyu law, after the initiation a boy is no longer a boy, but

86

a man in the fullness of his rights. On the other hand a girl, even when circumcised, does not become entitled to new rights."

(b) Women have no elder. (*Mongo, Zaïre*)

5. A woman can't become a man. (*Mamprusi, Burkina Faso*)

= "A commoner cannot become a prince. You can't change the status you have at birth."

6. Even small, man is old. (*Minyanka, Mali*)

= "The superiority of the male sex is not discussed. At least such it seems in public. A woman will never openly rebel against her husband. Man is always the first, even as a young boy."

7. Woman's intelligence is that of a child. (*West Africa, e.g. Benin, Senegal*)

8. A woman and an invalid man are the same thing. (*Gikuyu, Kenya*)

9. The male branch has priority. (*Mongo, Zaïre*)

= "Thus, for instance, the mother cannot receive the daughter's dowry, when the father is not there."

10. The pipe is right, the tobacco is wrong. (*Luba, Zaïre*)

11. A woman is like a goat: she is tethered where the thistles grow. (*Rwanda, Rwanda*)

= "A woman has to be treated harshly."

12. If a man is not obeyed by his wife, he must beat her, thwack! (*Swahili, East Africa*)

13. The arrogant woman is controlled by strokes. (*Rundi, Burundi; Rwanda, Rwanda*)

14. If you stumble upon a brawling couple, don't interrupt; only the husband knows what the wife has done to him. (*Ashanti, Ghana*)

15. Beat your wife regularly; if you don't know why, she will. (*West Africa, possibly of Arab origin*)

16. The better to beat his wife, the little man wears short clothes. (*Fon, Benin*)

= "Useless coming and going, excess of diligence; lots of noise, little effect."

17. A woman beaten for misbehaviour says: "Only she without one can ridicule me." (*Rwanda, Rwanda*)

= Without vagina, that is.

18. One cannot beat another's wife. (*Mongo, Zaïre*)

= "Juridical saying: if somebody else's wife has wronged you, you have to bring the case before her husband who alone has the right to punish her."

19. A wife is a piece of cloth; beat it and cover it at the same time. (*Mongo, Zaïre*)

20. Do not beat a wife with a stick but with food and clothes. (*Swahili, Kenya*)

21. A slap does not get a woman. (*Mamprusi, Burkina Faso*)

= "Rough behaviour is not profitable nor successful."

22. The stick that a woman cuts never crossed a river. (*Kru, Liberia*)

= "A woman cannot be the head of the family."

23. If a woman can bridge a river, a man can bridge the world. (*Mandinka, Senegal*)

= "Both are impossible."

24. Women have no mouth. (*Beti, Cameroon*)

25. No woman is called upon to speak. (*Rwanda, Rwanda*)

26. (a) Two cocks do not crow on the same roof. (*Mongo, Zaïre*)
(b) Two men cannot live in the same house. (*Rundi, Burundi*)

= "Quoted when a woman wants to dominate her husband."

27. The hen knows when it is morning, but she looks at the mouth of the cock. (*Ashanti, Ghana*)

= She waits for the cock to crow, as she should.

28. Women judge well in private matters, not in public. (*Kongo, Zaïre*)

29. (a) Your duty to your wife does not end with a cloth. (*Baule, Ivory Coast*)

(b) The buying of a wife begins from a little thing. (*Gikuyu, Kenya*)
(c) Marriage is more than paying the dowry. (*Kundu, Cameroon*)

30. No good for a man to owe a debt to a woman. (*Kundu, Cameroon*)

31. Do not lend three things: power, a wife, a gun. (*Fulani, Senegal*)

= "One does not lend them, because one would have difficulty in getting them back."

32. A woman in trousers? What's dangling inside? (*Fon, Benin*)

= "Why are these women meddling? Everybody has his own attributes."

33. One is cramped for room with a bad husband. (*Rundi, Burundi*)

= "Complaint of a badly married woman who cannot bloom because of the fidgety character of her husband."

34. The stick of a girl is "Touch-me-and-I-am-gone". (*Rwanda, Rwanda*)

= This is her means of defence. "For a trifle a wife abandons her husband."

35. Divorcing one, she is marrying one. (*Mamprusi, Burkina Faso*)

= "If a woman wants to divorce, she will either return to her father or go to another husband.
> A dependent has no alternative but to rely on someone else."

36. Only a shameful wife takes her husband to court. (*Ganda, Uganda*)

37. The strength of women is nothing but talk. (*Hausa, Niger/ Nigeria*)

38. A wife is a panther in your own bed. (*Umbundu, Angola*)

= "At home woman is the queen, the one who is in charge."

39. Woman is a spring in which all calabashes break. (*Cameroon*)

40. Virility gone, one might as well be woman. (*Rundi, Burundi*)

= "Said by someone who is aware of his decay, downfall, uselessness, impotence."

41. When the men have left the village, the women will bathe outside. (*Baule, Ivory Coast*)

42. When the women are fat and the men thin, the men will talk at the border of the fields. (*Fulani, Senegal*)

= "If the women have succeeded in becoming richer and stronger than the men, the latter won't dare deliberate in the village [where the women are] on strategies to end this abnormal situation, but they will hold their palavers outside the village with no women around.
> If some subjects have become too powerful, the chiefs discuss possible ways of getting their power back, but they do this secretly, and not publicly."

SOURCES

Oral Sources*

Ahmed Sheik Nabhani (Kenya): **II**. II, 10; X, 20
Almeida, Irène d' (Benin): **II**. X, 7, 15
Appiah, Peggy (Ghana): **I**. III, 13; **II**. VI, 12, 34; VIII, 29
Blondé-Nguluwe, Rosalinde (Namibia): **II**. IV, 7, 29
Duodu, Cameron (Ghana): **II**. I, 5
Eno-Belinga, Samuel Martin (Cameroon): **I**. III, 16; IV, 1; **II**. I, 14;
     III, 32; VI, 1
Faïk-Nzuji Madiya, Clémentine (Zaïre): **I**. II, 1ab, 2, 12; IV, 27, 28;
     VI, 2a; **II**. VIII, 13; X, 10
Funcke, Angelika von (German Federal Republic): see Werner
Gacheche Waruingi (Kenya): **I**. IV, 29, 30; V, 41a; **II**. VIII, 8, 15
Geschiere, Peter (Netherlands): see Vincent
Jeyifo, Biodun (Nigeria): **I**. III, 34; V, 28; **II**. 5, 17b
Jones, Eldred (Sierra Leone): **I**. IV, 7; V, 7, 43; **II**. X, 22
Ma Song, Rosalie (Burkina Faso): **II**. VII, 6
Makward, Edris (Senegal): **II**. VIII, 26c
Mboyi, Elisabeth (Zaïre): **I**. II, 12; **II**. III, 22; IX, 1
Mnthali, Felix (Malawi): **I**. II, 29
Mnyandu, Veli (South Africa): **I**. V, 5; **II**. VI, 32
Mugo, Micere Githae (Kenya): **I**. III, 11
N'Diaye, Papa Guèye (Senegal): **I**. III, 1; V, 3; **II**. II, 6; VIII, 20
Negash, Ghirmai (Ethiopia): **I**. I, 1; **II**. II, 1g
Schadeberg, Thilo (German Federal Republic): see Valente
Schoffeleers, Mathieu (Netherlands): **I**. V, 8a; **II**. VIII, 12a
Simonse, Simon (Netherlands): **I**. III, 39d
Soulé, Issiaka Adissa (Benin): **II**. VII, 19; VIII, 7d, 26a, 34, 35; IX,
     15

Source of all Evil

Tlali, Miriam (South Africa): **I**. V, 29; **II**. I, 6
Wembah-Rashid, John (Tanzania): **I**. V, 2; **II**. I, 11, 12

Written Sources**

Andrzejewski: **I**. III, 17:102; **II**. VIII, 33:152
Arbelbide: **I**. I, 3:34; II, 5ab:85; III, 10a:62; V, 6:82; VIII, 14:56;
    IX, 3:157; X, 5a:44; 23:101; **II**. II, 4:173; III, 2:188; 20:126;
    28:128; IV, 12:156; 14a:112; 14b:113; 21:181; 23:158; VI, 23:111;
    VIII, 22:86; IX, 4:141; X, 29a:30; 41:114
Areje: **I**. IV, 7:46; **II**. II, 1:44; 16:44; 17a:45; VI, 19:45; VII, 1:45
Bamgbose: **II**. IX, 9:75
Bantu Wisdom: **II**. 6b:38; 8:24; III, 14:51; 15:62; IV, 9:16; V, 9:12;
    10:12; 24ab:14; 33a:11; 35:30; VII, 13:58; **II**. I, 22:49; II, 2:48;
    9:63; III, 24:63; 33:62; IV, 1:62; 19:21; 35:15; VII, 22:23; X, 1:16
Barra: **I**. II, 4:62; 6a:92; III, 18:2; 28:12; V, 23b:11; IX, 4:29; X,
    6:50; 17:111; 21:16; 24:60; **II**. II, 12:121; III, 18:50; 30:59; IV,
    22:11; 37:44; V, 9:61; 15:71; VI, 11:86; VII, 3:19; 4:20; 5b:46;
    21:48; VIII, 10:2; X, 4:109; 8:71; 29b:5
Beken: **I**. II, 19ab:68; III, 12:65; IV, 2:66; 26:69; VII, 4:73; **II**. VI,
    15:75
Bon/Colin: **II**. I, 23:90; VI, 35:95
Cauvin (1980): **I**. I, 18:211; 19:541; 22:687; II, 26:60; III, 29:286;
    VII, 7:536; VII, 1:577; 7:544; 9:221; X, 7:239; 12:188; 13:284;
    14:453; 16:126; 20:525; 28:289; **II**. III, 9:374: 14a:342; 19:519;
    26:221; 27:569; 31:434; IV, 9:202; V, 12:61; 16:204; VI, 25:522;
    29:78; VIII, 31a:671; 31b:258: X, 6;525
Cauvin (1981): **I**. IV, 10:95; VII, 7:21; X, 4:80; 16:23; **II**. IX, 11:39
Crépeau/Bizimana: **I**. I, 5:101 and 487; 7:488; 8:345; 9:155; 10:487;
    16:208; 24:373; II, 22:476; 23:339; IV, 19:427; 22:478; 23:486; V,
    19:122; 20:525; 44a:460; VI, 5:488; 7:461; 8:350; 10:271; 11:75;
    12:205; 13:381; 14:380; 15:345; X, 8:43; 19:487; 25:43; **II**. I, 1:368;
    II, 3:476; 8:546; 13:452; 14:488; 15:195; 18:134; III, 8:477; 10:488;
    11:329; 13:444; 16:340; IV, 2:82; 4:177; 25:381; V, 2:578; 5:255;
    VI, 13a:541; 13b:392; 17:44; 24:382; VII, 8a:551; 18:477; VIII,
    5a:474; 5b:475; 18:223; 23:475; 26b:581; 30:448; IX, 5:478;
    13:425; X, 11:476; 13:478; 17:474; 25:339; 34:43
Dugast: **II**. VII, 8b:23–24
Faïk-Nzuji (1986a): **I**. I, 25a:11
Faïk-Nzuji (1986b): **I**. IV, 12:14
Finnegan: **I**. I, 6:406; II, 11:406; **II**. I, 19a:419

Gaden: **I**. II, 10:16; 18:15; III, 31:29; 35:37; IV, 17:70; V, 3:38; VII, 6:36; IX, 2:117; 5:305; X, 3:252; 26:230f; 29:21; **II**. I, 10:92; IV, 3:27; 8:252; 17:299; 20:142; VI, 2:37; 31:33; VII, 13:33; 19:54; VIII, 3c:15; 6, 7a:16; 7b:15; 25:21; 28:15; 32:22; X, 31:63; 42:80

Hofmayr: **I**. III, 9:377

Holas: **II**. III, 14b:84

Hulstaert: **I**. II, 9:600; 15a:133; III, 39b:643; IV, 3:643; 6:647; 20:647; 21:369; V, 4:376; 38a:434; 44b:354; **II**. I, 16:366; 21:646; IV, 10:625; V, 4:388; VII, 10:211; VIII, 1:132; X, 9:481; 18:523; 19:646; 26a:511

Issa/Labatut: **I**. II, 7:53; VII, 3:38; IX, 2:46

Ittmann: **I**. IV, 4:139; V, 27:124; 39:71; VI, 16:38; VIII, 3:7; 10:85; 11ab, 12, 13:96; **II**. I, 15:34; II, 7b:34; IV, 27:92; 28:22; VII, 15:91; VIII, 3b:11; 12b:60; X, 29c:35; 30:83

Jablow: **I**. III, 38:126; V, 3:127; 24b:126; 40:123; **II**. I, 19a:127; VI, 1:127; 4:127; VIII, 11:127

Jacquot: **I**. I, 4:76; VII, 9:81

Kalugila/Lodhi: **I**. III, 39a:32

Knappert: **I**. I, 23:196; **II**. VI, 14:197

Kouavi: **II**. II, 11:126; III, 34:137; VI, 21:117; X, 16:69; 32:83

Kuzwayo: **I**. V, 5:263

Lindfors/Owomeyola: **I**. III, 26:12; V, 1:28; 43:28; **II**. VI, 20:30; VII, 20:70; VIII, 3a:55; 21:30; 27:61

Meyer/Camara/Camara: **I**. III, 3:30; IV, 14:24; V, 11:58; IX, 7:148; **II**. III, 5:67; 21a:128; IV, 9:22; X, 23:56

Milimo: **I**. II, 6b:69; 15b:22; 17:91; **II**. VIII, 7c:116; X, 1:24

Ngumbu: **I**. I, 13:76; II, 13:1; V, 12:42; 13:47; 30:99; 32:60; VI, 1:84; 3:84; **II**. III, 30:71; IV, 31:79; VII, 5b:59

Njoku: **I**. VIII, 4:69

Ntahokaja: **I**. VII, 8:56

Nyembezi: **I**. I, 11:214; 21:230

Obenga: **I**. V, 33b:290; 36b:284; **II**. V, 3:299

Oduyoye: **II**. VI, 33 and 34:7; X, 14:9; 27:7

Ojoade: **II**. IX, 15:86

Parker: **II**. IV, 36:283; X, 3:282

Pelling: **I**. I, 6:17; 11:47; 15:29; III, 39c:41; VII, 12:42

Penfield; **I**. II, 25:112; X, 15:61; **II**. VI, 18:119; VIII, 19:59

Plissart: **I**. II, 27:102; III, 2:211; 5:225; 30:387; IV, 7:344; 16:130; VIII, 6:276; IX, 1:121; X, 1:121; 9:212; 10:310; 27:84; **II**. III, 12:70; 17:57; 23:258; 25:299; IV, 11:157; 15:153; V, 13:77; VII, 11a:325; 11b:407; VIII, 16:422; IX, 6:419; 10:332; 12:67; X, 5:103; 21:286; 35:299

Rattray: **I**. II, 30:140; III, 13:139; 20:139; IV, 31:139; **II**. I, 8:132; VI, 34:133; X, 14:139–140

Rodegem: **I**. I, 2:297; 17:53; III, 7:15; 24a:121; 24b:137; 27:192; IV, 15:366; 18:255; V, 15:318; 22:328; 31:308; 37:203; 44b:196; VI, 4:297; VII, 2:224; 10:78; X, 5b:346; 11:305; 22:96; **II**. I, 9:46; 24:90; IV, 16a:318; 16b:256; 26:317; V, 7:74; VI, 3:290; 8:109; 22:353; 30:291; VII, 12:92; VIII, 17:291; IX, 3:109; 7:292; X, 13:292; 26b:26; 33:285; 40:233

Roy/Daeleman: **I**. I, 25b:26; II, 21:9; VI, 6:65; **II**. VI, 5:47; VII, 2:13; IX, 1:17; X, 28:9

Sano: **I**. I, 12:49; III, 4:49; **II**. IV, 33:49

Scheven: **I**. I, 8:485; II, 14:488; 24:489; IV, 5:486; VII, 1:13; **II**. I, 2a:485; 7ab:485; III, 1:486; VII, 16:489; X, 12:487

Spagnolo: **II**. III, 15:352

Szwark: **I**. II, 28:116; III, 6:29; 10b:76; VIII, 2 and 8:68; **II**. I, 18:59; III, 3:116; VIII, 14:60; 24:60

Thomas: **I**. V, 18:743; **II**. III, 4:760; 29:762; IV, 13:758; X, 2ab:750; 2c:748

Travélé: **II**. III, 21b:46

Valente: **I**. II, 20:43; **II**. IX, 8:77; X, 38:44

Vincent: **II**. X, 24:75

Vissers: **I**. III, 36:20; 37:27; X, 18:9; **II**. VII, 14:19

Walser: **I**. I, 14:286; 20:419; II, 3:370; 16:372; III, 19:372; 21:114; 22:338; 23:258; 32:487; 33ab:372; IV, 8:196; 13:255; 24:420; 25:385; V, 8b:393; 14:64; 16:125; 17:284; 21:399; 23a:396; 25:304; 26:395; 34:61; 36a:357; 38b:393; VI, 2b:268; 9:68; VIII, 5:256; X, 2:372. **II**. I. 3:4; 17:260; 19b:381; 20:381; II, 7a:439; III, 7:372; IV, 5:143; 6:68; 18:287; 24:373; 30:143; 32:68; 34:71; V. 1:36; 6:373; 8:398; 10:372; 11:294; 14:393; VI, 6:115; 7 and 9:373; 16:452; 27:373; VII, 9:393; VIII, 4:372; 9:373; IX, 14:472; X, 36:189

Werner: **I**. IV, 33:327

Whitting: **I**. II, 29:94; III, 8:92; 25:95; IV, 32:179; 11:94; IX, 6:179; **II**. I, 4:94; VIII, 7b:54; X, 37:13

* The bold type **I** and **II** refer to Parts One and Two; the other Roman numerals refer to the various headings in *Phases of Life* and *Elements of Life*. The Arabic numerals correspond with the proverb numbers.

** The numbers after the colon signs refer to the corresponding pages in the written sources. For further references on these sources, see bibliography.

BIBLIOGRAPHY

Andrzejewski, B.W., and I.M. Lewis, *Somali Poetry: An Introduction*, Oxford: Clarendon Press, 1964.

Arbelbide, Cyprien, *Les Baoulés d'après leurs dictons et proverbes*, Abidjan: Céda, 1975.

Areje, Raphael Adekunle, *Yoruba Proverbs*, Ibadan: Daystar, 1985.

Bamgbose, Ayo, "The form of Yoruba proverbs", *Odu: University of Ife Journal of African Studies*, Vol.4, no. 2, January 1968, pp. 74–86.

Bantu Wisdom, A Collection of Proverbs, produced by the African Way of Life Club, Mchinchi (Malawi): Kachebere Major Seminary, 1969.

Barbier, Jean-Claude (ed.), *Femmes du Cameroun: Mères pacifiques, femmes rebelles*, Paris: Orstom/Karthala, 1985.

Barra, G., *1000 Kikuyu Proverbs*, Nairobi: Kenya Literature Bureau, 1939, 1984.

Beken, Alain van der, *Proverbes et vie yaka*, St Augustin 1, Anthropos-Institut, 1978.

Bon, Michel, and Roland Colin, "Les proverbes facteurs de développement", *Développements et Civilisations*, 41–2, Sept.–Dec. 1970, pp. 83–123,

Brookman-Amisah, J., "Some observations on the proverbs of the Akan-speaking peoples of Ghana", *Afrika und Übersee*, Band LV, 1971–2, pp. 262–7.

Carrington, John F., *Talking Drums of Africa*, London: Carey Kinsgate Press, 1949.

Cauvin, Jean, *L'image, la langue et la pensée. I: L'Exemple des proverbes (Mali); II: Recueil de proverbes Karangasso*, St Augustin 1, Anthropos-Institut, 1980.

Cauvin, Jean, *Comprendre les proverbes*, Saint-Paul: Editions Issy-les-Moulineaux, 1981.

Crépeau, Pierre, and Simon Bizimana, *Proverbes du Rwanda*, Tervuren: Musée Royal de l'Afrique Centrale, 1979.

Cutrufelli, Maria Rosa, *Women in Africa: Roots of Oppression*, London: Zed Press, 1983.

Dugast, Idelette, *Contes, proverbes, devinettes des Banen*, Paris: SELAF, 1975.

Faïk-Nzuji Madiya, Clémentine, *Les droits de la personne dans les proverbes africains*, Louvain-la-Neuve: Ciltade, 1, 1986.

Faïk-Nzuji, in collaboration with Balila Balu, *Les secrets de la parole sculptée*, Louvain-la-Neuve: Ciltade, 7, 1986.

Finnegan, Ruth, *Oral Literature in Africa*, Oxford: Clarendon Press, 1970.

Gaden, Henri, *Proverbes et maximes Peuls et Toucouleurs (traduits, expliqués et annotés)*, Paris: Institut d'Ethnologie, 1931.

Hamutyinei, M.A., and A.B. Plangger, *Tsumo-Shumo: Shona Proverbial Lore and Wisdom*, (Salisbury) Harare: Mambo Press, 1974.

Hofmayr, Wilhelm, *Die Schilluk: Geschichte, Religion und Leben eines Niloten-Stammes*, St Gabriel/Mödling: Bibliothèque Ethnologique Anthropos, 1925.

Holas, Bohumil, "Proverbe, expression de la sagesse populaire bété", *Notes africaines*, 119, 1968, pp. 83–8.

Hulstaert, G., *Proverbes Mongo,* Tervuren; Musée Royal du Congo belge, 1958.

Issa, Amadou, and Roger Labatut, *Sagesse des Peuls Nomades*, Yaoundé: Editions CLE, 1973.

Ittmann, Johannes, *Sprichwörter der Kundu (Kamerun)*, Berlin: Akademie-Verlag, 1971.

Jablow, Alta, *Yes and No: The Intimate Folklore of Africa*, Westport: Greenwood Press, 1961.

Jacquot, A., *Etudes béembe (Congo), Esquisse linguistique: Devinettes et proverbes*, Paris: Orstom, 1981.

Kalugila, L., and A.Y. Lodhi, *More Swahili Proverbs from East Africa*, Uppsala: Scandinavian Institute of African Studies, 1980.

Knappert, Jan, *Namibia, Land and Peoples, Myths and Fables*, Leiden: E.J. Brill, 1981.

Knappert, Jan, *The A–Z of African Proverbs*, London: Karnak House, 1989.

Kouaovi, Ahlin Bernard Mathias, *Proverbes et dictons du Bénin*, Porto-Novo: Protection du Patrimoine Culturel (PPC), 1981.

Kuzwayo, Ellen, *Call Me Woman*, London: The Women's Press, 1985.

Lindfors, Bernth O., and Oyekan Owomeyola, *Yoruba Proverbs: Translation and Annotation*, Athens, Ohio: Center for International Studies, 1973.

Meier-Pfaller, Hans-Josef (ed.), *Das grosse Buch der Sprichwörter*, Esslingen am Neckar: Bechtle Verlag, 1980.

Meyer, Gérard, with the collaboration of J.-R. Camara and F. Camara, *Proverbes malinké: A l'ombre des grands fromagers*, Paris: Edicef, 1985.

Milimo, J.T., *Bantu Wisdom*, Lusaka: Neczar, 1972.

Mukarovsky, Jan, Prislovi jako soucast kontextu ("Proverbs as a part of context"). Selected passages (translated by P.L. Garvin), in: Penfield, 1983, pp. 96–104.

Ngumbu Njururu, *Gikuyu Proverbs* (with English translation), Nairobi: Oxford University Press (1983), 1984.

Njoku, John E. Eberegbulam, *A Dictionary of Igbo Names, Culture and Proverbs*, Washington, DC: University Press of America, 1978.

Nketia, J.H. Kwabena, *The Music of Africa*, London: Victor Gollancz, 1979.

Ntahokaja, Jean-Baptiste, "La création littéraire dans la région des grands lacs", in: *Actes du Colloque de Bujumbura: La civilisation ancienne des peuples des grands lacs*, Paris/Bujumbura: Editions Karthala/Centre de Civilisation Burundaise, 1981.

Nyembezi, C.L. Sibusio, *Zulu Proverbs*, Johannesburg: Witwatersrand University Press, 1963.

Obenga, Théophile, *Littérature traditionelle des Mbochi (Congo-Afrique Centrale)*, Paris: Présence Africaine, 1984.

Obbo, Christine, *African Women: Their Struggle for Economic Independence*, London: Zed Press, 1981.

Oduyoye, Amba, "The Asante woman: socialization through proverbs", *African Notes*, Vol. VIII, no. 1, 1979, pp. 5–11.

Ojoade, J. Olowo, "Proverbs as a mirror of traditional Birom life and thought", in: Elizabeth Isichei (ed.), *Studies in the History of Plateau State, Nigeria*, London, Macmillan, 1982, pp. 85–9.

Oppong, Christine (ed.), *Female and Male in West Africa*, London, Allen & Unwin, 1983.

Bibliography

Oyesakin, Adefioye, "Women as agents of indiscipline in Yoruba traditional poetry", *Nigeria Magazine*, Vol. 53, no. 3, July–Sept. 1985, pp. 38–43.

Parker, Enid, "Afar stories, riddles and proverbs", *Journal of Ethiopian Studies*, Vol. IX, no.2, pp. 219–87.

Pelling, J.N., *Ndebele Proverbs and Other Sayings*, (Salisbury) Harare: Mambo Press, 1977.

Penfield, Joyce, *Communicating with Quotes: The Igbo Case*, Westport/London: Greenwood Press, 1983.

Penguin Dictionary of Proverbs, The, Harmondsworth: Penguin Books, (1983), 1985.

Plissart, Xavier, *Mamprusi Proverbs*, Tervuren: Musée Royal de l'Afrique Centrale, 1983.

Rattray, R.S., *Ashanti Proverbs*, Oxford: Oxford University Press, 1916.

Rodegem, F.M. (ed), *Sagesse kirundi: Proverbes, dictons, locutions usités au Burundi*, Tervuren: Musée Royal du Congo Belge, 1961.

Rosaldo, Michelle Zimbalist, and Louise Lamphere (eds.), *Woman, Culture and Society*, Stanford University Press, 1985.

Roy, H. van, and J. Daeleman, *Proverbes Kongo*, Tervuren: Musée Royal de l'Afrique Centrale, 1963.

Sano, Mohamed Lamine, "Proverbes", *Littérature guinéenne*, Special issue of *Notre Librairie*, 88/89, July-September 1987, pp. 44–9.

Scheven, Albert, *Swahili Proverbs: Nia zikiwa moja, kilicho mbali huja*, Washington, DC: University Press of America, 1981.

Schipper, Mineke (ed.), *Unheard Words: Women and Literature in Africa, the Arab World, Asia, the Caribbean and Latin America*, London: Allison & Busby, 1985.

Sklovski, V., "L'art comme procédé", in: T. Todorov, *Théorie de la littérature*, Paris: Seuil, 1966, pp.76–97.

Spagnolo, Rev. Fr L.M., *Bari Grammar*, Verona: Missioni Africane, 1933.

Szwark, Marian, *Proverbes et traditions des Bassars du Nord Togo*, St Augustin 1, Anthropos-Institut, Hans Völker und Kulturen, 1981.

Thomas, Jacqueline M., *Ngbaka-Ma'bo (République Centrafricaine) Contes, Proverbes, Devinettes ou Enigmes, Chants et Prières*, Paris: Klincksieck, 1970.

Travélé, Moussa, *Proverbes et Contes Bambara (Bambara et Malinké)*, Paris: Paul Geuthner, (1923), 1977.

Valente, P. José Francisco, *Selecçâo de provérbios e adivinhas em Umbundu*, Lisboa: Junta de Investigaçoes do Ultramar, 1964.

Vincent, J. F., *Traditions et transitions: Entretiens avec des femmes beti du Sud-Cameroun*, Paris: Orstom, Berger/Lerrault.

Vissers, Jan, *Spreekwoordenboek in Beeld: Een aparte kunst uit Cabinda*, Berg en Dal, Afrika Museum, 1982.

Walser, Ferdinand, *Luganda Proverbs*, Berlin: Reimer Verlag, 1982.

Werner, Roland, *Grammatik des Nobiin (Nilnubisch): Phonologie, Tonologie und Morphologie*, Hamburg: Helmet Buske Verlag, 1987.

Whitting, C.E.J., *Hausa and Fulani Proverbs*, Lagos: Government Printer, 1940.